D0570924

Dear Emily,
 Although we didn't get to see much of
Amsterdam we hope that this book can
be a reminder for you of our North Atlantic
cruise with you on the M.S. Rotterdam in 2003.

AMSTERDAM

By Hans Koning
and the Editors of Time-Life Books

Photographs by Patrick Ward

With love,

Grandma and Grandpa
Girdner

THE GREAT CITIES · TIME-LIFE BOOKS · AMSTERDAM

The Author: Hans Koning, the pen name of novelist Hans Koningsberger, grew up on Wouwermanstraat in Amsterdam. During the Second World War he escaped to England and served in the British Army. In 1951 he settled in the United States to pursue a writing career. Among his best-known novels, some of which he helped make into films, are *The Affair, The Revolutionary, A Walk with Love and Death* and *The Petersburg-Cannes Express*. He has written a number of travel books, including *Love and Hate in China* and *A New Yorker in Egypt*.

The Photographer: Patrick Ward was born in London in 1937. His work has been featured in many English newspapers and magazines, and he has contributed to a British Council travelling exhibition. His pictures for "The English at Play", a one-man show at the Photographers Gallery in London, appeared in the book *Wish You Were Here*, published by Gordon Fraser.

Editor: George Constable
Design Consultant: Louis Klein
Director of Photography: Pamela Marke

Editorial Staff for Amsterdam
Deputy Editor: Windsor Chorlton
Designer: Graham Davis
Picture Editor: Jasmine Spencer
Staff Writers: Mike Brown, Norman Kolpas, Deborah Thompson
Researcher: Vanessa Kramer
Design Assistants: Shirin Patel, Fiona Preston

Editorial Production for the Series
Art Department: Julia West
Editorial Department: Ellen Brush, Molly Sutherland
Picture Department: Thelma Gilbert, Brigitte Guimpier, Christine Hinze

The captions and the texts accompanying the photographs in this volume were prepared by the editors of TIME-LIFE Books.

Valuable assistance was given in the preparation of this volume by Jeanne Buys, Amsterdam.

Published by TIME-LIFE International (Nederland) B.V. Ottho Heldringstraat 5, Amsterdam 1018.

© 1977 TIME-LIFE International (Nederland) B.V. All rights reserved. Second English printing, 1978.

No part of this book may be reproduced in any form or by any electronic or mechanical means, including information storage and retrieval devices or systems, without prior written permission from the publisher, except that brief passages may be quoted for review.

ISBN 7054 0487 0

Cover: Steeply pitched tile roofs with graceful gable ends embellish a row of 17th-Century houses that overlook the Keizersgracht, one of Amsterdam's principal canals.

First end paper: Neat stacks of Dutch clogs, or *klompen*, are offered for sale in one of the three remaining Amsterdam workshops that make them. The painted clogs are destined for the tourist shopper; the plain ones are bought by a few tradition-minded Dutchmen who regard them as the ideal footwear for staying dryshod in muddy fields and gardens.

Last end paper: A pair of convex mirrors, set into a wall of the Herengracht to guide canal-boat traffic safely around a tight turn, reflect peaceful vistas at the heart of Amsterdam.

Contents

I

The Open City

In a city that doesn't boast a single hill, there is special pleasure to be had in taking a bird's-eye look at streets, houses and canals that one normally views only from ground level. That is why, when arranging to see a friend shortly after the start of my latest stay in Amsterdam, I suggested we meet in a restaurant on the top floor of the 13-storey Harbour Building—a veritable eyrie by local standards. To make the most of the opportunity, I arrived well ahead of the appointed time and spent long minutes studying the panoramic scene: the old city centre spread out below, built of mellow brick and stone three centuries ago; the 19th-Century and early 20th-Century town beyond, with its gridlike arrangement of apartment houses and office blocks; and away in the far distance, houses, roads, fields and water losing themselves in sea-mists.

I had never enjoyed this particular view before, although much of what I saw is a part of me. Born and raised an Amsterdammer, I had left the city a few years after the Second World War, one of a last group of Dutchmen to embark—for one reason or another—on a voyage to Indonesia, formerly the Dutch East Indies: at the time there was still a close relationship between Holland and the one-time colony that had gained independence in 1949. I spent a year doing radio work in the Far East and then settled in the United States to pursue a writing career. Since then, I had returned to Amsterdam only for short visits. But this time I was to write about the city: I would have to see how much it had changed, and it seemed appropriate that I should begin my stay by observing Amsterdam in a new perspective. I cannot, of course, claim perfect objectivity. One wisdom I've learned from all my wanderings is the truth of the poet Horace's words: *Coelum non animum mutant qui trans mare currunt* ("Travelling changes your sky, but not your mind"). It loses in translation.

The harbour below me, for all its modern piers and basins, didn't look very different from the harbour I grew up with: it was the same waterscape, full of glittering, shifting parallels of blue and grey that compelled the eye to seek out the one line defining the edge of the earth. But the Harbour Building itself, built in 1960, was like nothing in the Amsterdam of my youth. The glass-and-concrete tower—supported by hundreds of concrete columns sunk to a depth of 80 feet in the muddy, waterlogged soil—stands out like a sore thumb against its venerable surroundings.

Amsterdam would be an easy place to spoil, I thought. Although it is the capital of the world's third most densely populated country, fewer than 800,000 people live within the municipality's 80 square miles. How much

From her vantage point on the roof of the Royal Palace, the Virgin of Peace gazes down on Dam Square, Amsterdam's favoured meeting-place for young people. The statue holds the Rod of Mercury and an olive branch, representing the city's twin ideals of trade and peace.

more vulnerable a city of this modest size must be to the sort of pressures that are turning some metropolises into nondescript sprawls of office blocks, motorways and housing developments. And Amsterdam faces another, more serious threat. The city sits an average 12 feet below sea level (Schiphol Airport, some seven miles from the town centre, was built on the site of a naval battle between Dutch and Spanish fleets in 1573) and, like Venice, all its old buildings stand on timber piles—an estimated five million of them. A 17th-Century verse expressed the Amsterdammers' misgivings about the future of their city:

The great town of Amsterdam stands on piles—until it falls down.
Who will pay the bill then?

The city council's annual outlay of the equivalent of tens of millions of dollars for preserving old structures partly justifies the pessimistic outlook of earlier generations of Amsterdammers. But the city's forefathers would no doubt consider the money well spent. In spite of such ominous portents as the Harbour Building, Amsterdam has resisted sweeping changes— physical ones at least—more successfully than most cities. In fact, the old town has changed little since the 17th Century, when Amsterdam was the capital of an enormous trading empire and one of the most influential cities in the world. If Rembrandt were to revisit the town where he spent the last 37 years of his life, he would have little difficulty finding his way around.

The old part of Amsterdam—a 17th-Century development surrounding the medieval core—is laid out in the shape of a fully opened fan, with its base along the harbour and its framework made up of three large concentric canals—the Herengracht, the Keizersgracht and the Prinsen-gracht—that are interconnected by hundreds of smaller waterways. Altogether, some 63 miles of canals are crammed into an area little more than one mile across. Within this semicircle—and fronting the narrow, cobbled streets and rows of elm and linden trees that run along the canals —is an extraordinary concentration of tall, slender houses. If I had to describe the district in one word, I would call it picturesque, in the sense of that word before it was ruined by misuse. This is a city worthy of being painted; a city that looks as if it was designed by painters.

As well-preserved as it is, the old part of the city is not merely an architectural museum. Many canalside houses, former homes of rich burghers who traded in spices from the Indies, are now occupied by the staffs of international corporations or by some of the 300 or so stockbroking firms that help make Amsterdam the fourth largest financial centre in the world. In other buildings diamond cutters—reputed to be the best in the world— continue a craft tradition that started in the 1580s when a few such artisans fled to Amsterdam from Antwerp to escape an invading Spanish army. In a sense, Amsterdammers have the best of two worlds. Their links with the past are strong, but the façades of the city centre hide all the trappings of a bustling, late 20th-Century metropolis.

A gaudily embellished barrel-organ, one of eight instruments that continue a long-standing Amsterdam tradition, lightens the step of passers-by near the Amstel. Unlike most of the other street organs, this one is operated by hand rather than a petrol-driven motor.

As the late afternoon twilight closed in over the harbour, I turned away from the window to face a waiter who informed me there were no tables to be had without a reservation. Just as well, I thought: this restaurant was not my kind of place; it was all a bit exaggerated, from the breathless modernity of the décor to the aloof air of the waiters and the prices on the multi-lingual menu. Too much *capsones* (pretentiousness), as Amsterdammers used to say of a person or institution with an inflated sense of importance. I felt a stab of nostalgia for the Bodega Keyzer café-restaurant, near the Concert Hall in the southern part of the old town, where my mother used to take me for dinner on Sunday evenings. The décor there—dark wood panelling and potted plants—was conservative, and the waiters un-obtrusively courteous. We would be greeted by "our" Mr. van Os, dressed always in black tie and tails, who would bring my mother a magazine or two to peruse while she had her coffee and I drank a hot chocolate. (Later, I found the Keyzer still in business, and not even greatly changed.)

Here, however, not even the customers seemed to fit memory's moulds. No couples sat sipping little glasses of Dutch gin; instead, an international crowd was talking over Scotches and Bloody Marys. I couldn't help wonder-ing if the Amsterdammers among them had managed as well as their city to retain their special character, which over the centuries has variously infuriated, delighted or baffled visitors. Almost without exception, early travellers to Amsterdam wrote of the stolidity of its inhabitants and their deep-dyed commercialism. At the same time, observers were amazed at the tolerance shown by Amsterdammers to the many immigrants who came to

Viewed from the air, Amsterdam's concentric canals seem to spread outwards in ripples from Dam Square, located behind the massive Royal Palace (centre).

ADAM WOOLFITT, SUSAN GRIGGS AGENCY, LONDON

escape religious persecution—Jews from Portugal, Spain and Poland, Protestants from Belgium, Huguenots from France. "It appears at first not to be a city of any particular people but to be common to all," a visitor to Amsterdam wrote in the 17th Century.

Since the Second World War, the Amsterdammers' character has seemed even more contradictory. In the 1960s visitors to the city were apprised of startling new developments when they found Dam Square, the city's main plaza, filled with hippies from all over the world and the air above them blue with marijuana smoke. In those years, visitors were likely to be merely bemused at the highly publicized activities of a group of local anarchists—known as Provos, short for "Provocateurs"—who were trying to make Amsterdam the capital of an alternative, non-technological culture. But bemusement turned to anxiety in the 1970s when Amsterdam was discovered to be the European centre for transactions in hard drugs. A British newspaper with a penchant for puns offered this scathing comment: "Can it really be true that Holland lies so low that it can only be saved by being damned?"

No, Amsterdammers are not damned—anymore than they are the plodding, humourless citizens of travellers' lore. In fact, I hold that they—more than any other city-dwellers I know—embody the essence of urban living: a love for the security of family, home and friends, tempered by a desire to be left alone, and to leave others alone.

One of the first visitors to notice the Amsterdammers' respect for privacy was the French philosopher René Descartes, who lived in the city during the 1630s. In 1631 he wrote to a friend in France, urging him to join him: "I suggest Amsterdam for your retirement . . . I could spend my entire life here without being noticed by a soul. I go for a walk every day in the Babel of a great thoroughfare as freely and restfully as you stroll in your garden."

Less flatteringly, Descartes attributed the Amsterdammers' indulgent attitude to a supposed infatuation with money so total that they had no attention to spare for other matters. This criticism was echoed vehemently by an Englishman 60 years later. "If you talk with one of their preachers about religion," he wrote, "he diverts you to trade, and still thinks himself upon the first topic—which is the only truth he is guilty of."

Being a born Amsterdammer, I can say with conviction that our so-called commercialism is an exaggeration, just as any Parisian knows there are plenty of Paris restaurants that serve mediocre food and plenty of Parisians who let whole days drift by without thinking about sex. I wouldn't deny, however, that this is, and always has been, a city of merchants. Since the 13th Century, when Amsterdam was merely a village clustered around a dam in the Amstel River—and thus known as Amstelredam—it has been a place of passage for men and goods from all over Europe; and from the turn of the 17th Century onwards, its cargo ships sailed as far as Japan to the east and America to the west.

Two near-casualties testify to the peculiar hazards of canalside parking. At left, a motor bike hangs with one wheel in the water, saved from total immersion only by its burglar-proof chain. Above, a car balances precariously against the landing stage of a houseboat, waiting to be hauled back to terra firma by the city fire brigade. Careless or unlucky owners must bear the cost of salvage operations.

The far-ranging nature of this trade surely helps explain the tolerance of Amsterdammers better than Descartes' notions about obsessive commercialism. As a result of the centuries of overseas trading, Amsterdam is infected with a healthy dose of internationalism—not the superficial internationalism of the chain-hotel bar or the airport lounge, mind you, but the internationalism of a population that is utterly dependent on commerce and travel. Citizens of Amsterdam have had to meet with men of all countries and customs while earning their living; have had to learn to accept them, to live with them; and often even to value them. A merchant or sailor or financier cannot afford to be exclusive, a jingo, or—literally—a stick-in-the-mud. Amsterdammers, in fact, have occasionally gone as far in the opposite direction as one could possibly go. For example, during a war between Holland and England in the late 18th Century, some citizens of the city were seen to be curiously unhappy when they received a report that the Dutch navy had won a victory over the British at Dogger Bank in the North Sea: it turned out that they had been underwriting the insurance policies for the British warships.

Amsterdammers have another intriguing dimension: their individualism, their refusal to conform—a quality that belongs to the Dutch in general but that is nowhere more evident than in Amsterdam. Nonconformism, too, can be tied in with the tradition of seafaring and foreign trading, for such activities—in contrast to the occupations of landlubbers—breed independent attitudes: "Town air makes free," Amsterdammers said in the 17th Century; "sea air makes freer." Perhaps their independent outlook goes back as far as the 13th and 14th Centuries when freemen—boat-builders, dike builders, fishermen and millers who worked for themselves, and who were not under the vassalage of local lords—migrated to Amsterdam from northern Holland, while other Dutch towns, such as Utrecht and Rotterdam, grew through influxes of peasants from feudal regions in the south and east.

Amsterdammers prize their independence so much that they rarely band together in a common cause. If your neighbour is against something, that is reason enough to assume a positive stance towards it. Amsterdammers cannot even form a united front on such a basic issue as religion. For instance, although Protestantism is nominally the religion of Holland, an Amsterdammer may belong to any one of 20 churches, divided from one another not only on questions of doctrine, but also on such matters as health inoculation, vivisection, and the role of women in politics. Amsterdam's Catholics are just as nonconforming. In the early 1970s they were in the forefront of a move to allow priests to marry; they attended experimental religious services where marijuana was smoked and pop music was played; and about 80 per cent chose to ignore the papal encyclical that forbade birth control.

In local politics, the situation is hardly more orderly. Elections for the 45 seats on the Municipal Council have, in recent years, seen candidates offered by upwards of a dozen parties, ranging from Catholic conservatives to far leftists to such special-interest groups as a "barrel-organ party" dedicated to preserving the mobile barrel-organs that have long been a part of Amsterdam tradition. Surely the most novel political faction of recent years has been the Kabouters, whose name translates as "elves" or "gnomes" and who represented a further evolution of the Provo move-ment of the 1960s. In one election, these "gnomes" issued a manifesto demanding the abolition of automobiles in the city (everyone was to be given a bicycle) and a return to self-sufficiency (farms were to be created on wasteland and their produce given to commune members). As for the environmental pollution caused by conventional means of generating power, the Kabouters' cure was crystal-clear: electricity would be produced by windmills built for every house.

I telephoned the man who was supposed to meet me at the Harbour Building restaurant to tell him there were no tables. Luckily I caught him in time, and he asked me to come instead to his home on the Keizersgracht, one of the three main canals that ring the old city and that are, together, its symbol. His house dates from the 17th Century and retains its original, weathered-brick façade, topped by a white-painted, bell-shaped gable. But the occupant was an architect, and it showed: inside, walls had been removed and low tables and freeform chairs were arranged in the large rooms. We sat at a ceiling-to-floor window and I looked out over water once more—this time the confined space of the canal surface, which reflected the soft glow of street lamps and the shapes of motionless trees.

I asked my friend for his assessment of tolerance in Amsterdam.

"This city is more than tolerant," he said quickly. "That's a word I haven't used in 20 years. Amsterdam is now an experimental town. Everything is up for discussion here. Every experiment can be tried."

When he spoke of experimentation, I knew that he meant changes in social attitudes as well as technological innovations. He himself is a non-conforming man, the president of C.O.C.—the Dutch Society for the Integration of Homosexuals. In 1972 the society, which has been campaigning openly since the 1940s, was granted government recognition. In the same year the architect was awarded a decoration by the government for his work, along with others, in promoting the aims of the C.O.C. "We managed to get homosexuals accepted into the army," he said. "Some of my friends are furious with me, but I tell them quite firmly that 'no discrimination' means *no discrimination*.

"But don't misunderstand me," he continued. "If homosexuals come here from other countries to live, and many do, it's not because they are liked in Amsterdam. We aren't liked. We aren't disliked. We are simply one more group among many. I get annoyed when people from abroad tell me this is a permissive town. The word implies that some people—the right ones, presumably—permit others to be different. What an insult!"

On the dark canal, a glass-roofed sightseeing boat appeared, throwing up a cone of light. The amplified voice of the tour guide manifested itself as a loud drone, but we could not distinguish a word. I waited until the boat had vanished under the next bridge, then returned to my original question.

"What I want to establish," I said, "is whether the various people who have come to live in Amsterdam over the centuries—religious exiles, Vietnam war deserters, Indonesians, and so on—ended up as Amsterdammers and made a contribution to the life of the city."

"They were and are accepted," the architect said, "if they had or have something of value to offer. But I think Amsterdam has been a truly tolerant society only since the Second World War. The shock of the German Occupation put an end to our smugness, to mindless cruelty towards our fellows."

I myself witnessed the traumas of the German Occupation, and when I returned to Amsterdam after the war, I noticed how the old established values had been shaken up. Apart from a new pride in their city (perhaps the reason why its inhabitants are prepared to pay the massive bill for its upkeep), Amsterdammers had pulled down many class barriers, including the one surrounding a person's address. In pre-war days, your address in Amsterdam defined your job, income and social status, and perhaps your father's and grandfather's before you. There was little social mobility. My father was born within walking distance of my birthplace; and both my grandfathers lived within walking distance of our house.

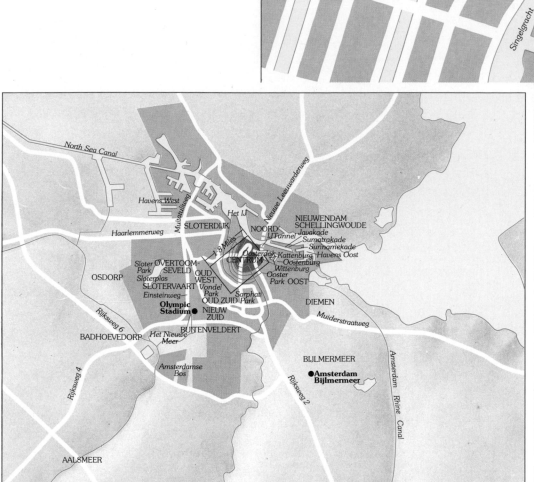

Amphibious Amsterdam

Lying several feet below sea level, Amsterdam is protected by a carefully maintained system of dikes and dams. The old part of the city (map at right), originated as a medieval fishing village along the banks of the Amstel River. It developed its semicircular layout in the 17th Century, when three great, concentric canals—the Herengracht, Keizersgracht and Prinsengracht—were dug as part of a network of waterways that enabled freight to be transported by barge to all parts of the sea-trading city.

Modern Amsterdam holds more than 750,000 people within its 80 square miles (inset map), almost a quarter of them living in suburbs linked by road and rail to a centre that has changed little in three centuries.

Westerkerk

Anne Frank House

Round Lutheran Church

Singel

Spuistraat

Nieuwezijds Voorburgwal

Central Station

De Ruijterkade

IJ

Raadhuisstraat

●Nieuwe Kerk

Nieuwendijk

Herengracht

Royal Palace

Damrak

Singel

Spuistraat

Dam

National Monument

Warmoesstraat

Schreierstoren

Nieuwezijds Voorburgwal

Historical Museum

Kalverstraat

●Oude Kerk

Rokin

Voorburgwal

Zeedijk

Oudezijds

Statue in Begijnhof

Oudezijds Achterburgwal

Spui

Nieuwmarkt

Trippenhuis

Weigh House

Prins Hendrikkade

Eilandsgracht

Muntplein

Kloveniersburgwal

Montelbaanstoren

Oosterdok

oren

St. Antoniesbreestraat

Oudeschans

Amstel

Rembrandt

AMSTEL RIVER

Rembrandt House

Waterlooplein

Rembrandtsplein

Thorbeckeplein

Herengracht

Moses and Aaron Church

Muiderstraat

Urechtsestraat

Jonas Daniel Meijerplein

●Portuguese synagogue

Dock worker

Nieuwe Herengracht

Wertheim Park

Hortus Botanicus

Magere Brug

Nieuwe Keizersgracht

Just as your address marked you, so did your speech: a single turn of phrase could place you. The speech shibboleths still exist, even more strongly than in Britain, but the snobbery surrounding addresses was eradicated by the desperate post-war housing shortage which compelled the authorities to distribute the available accommodations to the neediest, particularly families with two or more children; people with spare rooms were obliged to let them out to the homeless. Since then, although housing is still short, there have been so many regulations introduced—subsidies for house-buyers, an allocation to immigrants of 5 per cent of all new housing construction, redevelopment of run-down areas in accordance with plans worked out with the residents—that there can be no return to the pre-war pattern of segregation.

But in spite of Amsterdam's deserved reputation for its social welfare programmes, my latest visit had already shown me something that did not tally with my ideas about the city's tolerance. The day before, a young woman civil rights worker had advised me to go and see a boarding-house of Moroccan "guest workers" (the term is a somewhat painful euphemism in use throughout most of Western Europe for Mediterranean nationals who fill many menial jobs.) A walk down Jacob Catskade, a street of pleasant houses along a quiet canal in Amsterdam West, had brought me to the address. On the first floor, slightly above street level, I saw a Dutch couple sitting in a neat little living-room, watching television and reading. The boarding-house proved to be in the basement.

Once through the basement door, I was in a different world. Whoever has seen Jacob Riis's famous turn-of-the-century photographs of immigrants in New York City will never forget the misery they portray; here was a scene worthy of Riis. Thirteen beds were crowded into one long, unheated, windowless room; a single toilet had been built into a cupboard and there was a tiny kitchen. Each guest worker was paying a hundred guilders a month for his bed (the equivalent of about $40). Altogether, the landlord was making 1,300 guilders a month from this apartment—perhaps 10 times the rent of the couple living alone on the floor above. "The landlord," I now reported to my architect friend, "turned out to be Moroccan himself, but that's neither here nor there."

The architect was silent for a while, and then said, "I know about these rackets. All Amsterdammers do—which is not the same as seeing them for yourself. You will probably ask me, 'What about our splendid municipal housing ordinances that guarantee a certain amount of living space?' I can only reply that, because we leave people alone, don't intrude on personal privacy, don't tell people what they can or cannot do, and don't ask for their identity papers on street corners, such exploitation can go undetected. It's the price we pay for personal freedom."

What the architect told me about the compromise between personal freedom and the law was essentially similar to the explanations of a police

Strings of electric lights limn the Magere Brug (Skinny Bridge) over the Amstel River. Built nearly 300 years ago, the wooden drawbridge is still raised by hand.

ADAM WOOLFITT. SUSAN GRIGGS AGENCY. LONDON

officer whom I accompanied a few days later on his evening patrol in a Volkswagen police bus through the toughest part of town. He was a plain-clothes member of a special "summer visitors" detachment that operates from May to October—the height of the tourist season.

"We don't use the power of the city to make waves," he said to me. "We don't break up that boarding-house, because the Moroccans would only end up sharing with even more of their countrymen in another room. We don't arrest kids who take marijuana, because we know it wouldn't stop them or cure them of the habit."

While this policeman was a soft-spoken, sensible sounding man, I don't mean to imply that all Amsterdam police are like that. I met a colleague of his who enviously cited the machine pistols that German police carry in the door pockets of their cars: "That's the way to talk to these kids, with a machine pistol in your hand." Nevertheless, Amsterdam's prevailing attitude to the taking of so-called "soft drugs", particularly marijuana, is so lenient compared with the stand taken by other countries that it amazes foreign observers and scandalizes more conservative Dutchmen.

Although the law forbids possession of marijuana—whether as "grass", the dried leaves of *cannabis sativa*, or as concentrated extract (cannabis resin) the fines imposed on conviction are no more than an offender would get for parking illegally. Furthermore, each Saturday the commodity rates of the various types of soft drugs available in Amsterdam are broadcast on Hilversum Radio, together with advice on clinics that treat drug takers. Cannabis has even been smoked by council members within the hallowed chambers of the Town Hall, without police taking any action: after five Kabouters won election to the city council in 1970, they shocked their more conservative colleagues by "turning on" during a council session. Even if possession of marijuana is technically forbidden, there is no law against the growing of cannabis plants. A common sight on city houseboats is a window box or pot containing a luxurious growth of the plant for the owner's private use. And if actual cultivation of marijuana is too onerous, a person can always buy home-grown cannabis plants on a houseboat moored right opposite a police station.

We got out of the police bus in Amsterdam's red-light district, in the very heart of the old town, where neon signs advertise sexual aids and live sex shows that leave nothing to the imagination. As we walked down the Zeedijk, the main street of the district, the patrolman said, "Come, I'll show you something." He led me through an open door into an apartment house and up a narrow staircase. On the second-floor landing, a Chinese sat on a kitchen chair in a doorway. He knew the policeman and nodded to him. We looked past him. There were about a dozen Chinese inside the room, most of them lying on cots. They were all smoking pipes; and a strangely sweetish smell, unknown to me, filled the air. It was an opium den. No one paid any attention to us, except for a well-dressed man who came over to

A young couple concentrate on a chess game in the Catholic Moses and Aaron church on the Waterlooplein. Amsterdam's church authorities allowed it to be turned into a leisure centre for the young and a dormitory for the homeless, although the building remains a consecrated place of worship where services are held every Sunday morning.

shake hands and offer us cigars. We clambered down the stairs again. "There are many more dens like that in Amsterdam," the policeman said when we were outside. "We leave them alone, on condition they allow only Chinese in. It's better than forcing them underground."

In my childhood, many of the Chinese in Amsterdam were sailors who had jumped ship and were scraping a living by selling peanut brittle from trays they carried with straps slung around their necks; they were reputed to make this confection themselves, using spit in the process, and we called all Chinese "peanutmen". But those days are gone, and now Amsterdam's Chinese apparently control the sale of something far more dangerous—heroin. The Chinese community has been swollen by immigrants from Singapore and Hong Kong, and this influx has included members of the triads—secret underworld societies that have been called the "Chinese Mafia". These triads gained control of Amsterdam's drug market in the early 1970s, and rival gangs fought bitterly to win a monopoly of the heroin trade: Yong Fatt Tong, an underworld leader credited with making Amsterdam a drug smuggler's Mecca, was shot dead by members of a rival gang in 1975, and in the year after his death, three of his successors were murdered—all in Amsterdam.

While the city's police might countenance opium-smoking among the Chinese, they took a hard line towards heroin as its use increased dramatically in the mid-1970s. An estimated 5,000 to 10,000 addicts live in Amsterdam. Furthermore, the annual count of heroin addicts found dead of overdoses has been rising. Significantly, only a fraction of the victims tend to be Dutch; the rest are Europeans and Americans attracted to the city by the easy availability and low prices of the drug.

In the effort to stop the trafficking, tough new measures were introduced at the end of 1976, making possession of hard drugs punishable by a 12-year prison sentence. (Formerly, the maximum penalty was a four-year term.) But passing laws and enforcing them are two different things. During my patrol with the policeman, I saw for myself the difficulties that face both the local police and the Dutch Narcotics Squad. As we walked down the Zeedijk after visiting the opium den, the patrolman pointed out several cafés. "That's where they are dealing in hard drugs, heroin and cocaine," he said, "and there, and there."

"Can't you catch them?" I asked.

"We can't get enough proof. They know us all, of course. There are something like five exits to a place like that. All we can do is watch and wait and hope to catch them red-handed. It's the price we pay for not having the authority to check identities or frisk suspects without a search warrant."

Another reason why drug pedlars and drug supplies have poured into the city is that border formalities with neighbouring countries have been relaxed to the point where passports often go unchecked; the Netherlands is wide open. The patrolman told me how he and a colleague once took a

German junkie to the border in a police car, sent him across, and then stopped to have a cup of coffee. When they started back to Amsterdam, they passed the same fellow standing at the roadside, trying to hitch a lift back to Amsterdam. They did not bother to stop.

After our walk along the Zeedijk, the policeman and I sat in his Volkswagen bus for a while, until a message came through on the radio: a man in Vondel Park was bothering passers-by. The patrolman started the bus and drove fast through the town. Vondel Park, just south-west of Leidseplein (Leyden Square), is the equivalent of New York's Central Park. It is a pleasant place, free of traffic, with a lot of playgrounds, ponds and benches. On a warm day, girls sunbathe topless with no one staring at them; by night, people can walk or cycle there in safety. We drove into one of the park's wide pedestrian lanes, the pebbles crunching under the wheels. "There he is," the policeman said, steering across the grass to where a young man was standing. He wore an old raincoat, over clothes that were in disarray. The policeman stopped the bus and leaned out of the window.

"What's going on here?" he asked.

The young man just looked at him and blinked.

"Where are you from?"

"From Hooftstraat," the youth said finally, in an accent that I recognized as Amsterdam.

He was on a "speed trip", he confessed without hesitation. Where had he obtained the drugs? Oh, somewhere. No, he hadn't taken his trousers down; they were torn.

"Listen, you look like a nice boy," the policeman said. "Now, I want you to go home. Leave the park by the nearest exit, do you hear? If I see you in this condition again, I'll have to take you in."

The young man asked him in a hoarse whisper if he could have a cigarette. "No," the policeman said. "Here, take this," and he handed him the cigar he had been given at the opium den. He shrugged as we drove off. "I tell myself he won't be alive ten years from now, but what can we do? Young people are defenceless, aren't they?"

The policeman's patience with a fellow Amsterdammer may not be too surprising; but how well has the city's reputation for tolerance stood the test of the political refugees who arrived in the 1970s, and who also cause social problems? Among recent arrivals have been Kurds from Iran, a people who had been fighting a war against Iraq—where most of their homeland lies—until a deal between Iraq and Iran deprived them of both their traditional territory and their base in Iran.

Interestingly, once the Dutch government recognizes such people as the Kurds as genuine political refugees, they cannot be deported, and they will be given support money and a decent hotel room until they have found a job and can afford an apartment.

Earlier in the day I had visited a Kurdish refugee organization at their office in a stately building on the Herengracht (the government paid the rent). The house was a far cry from the shabby basement world of the Moroccan guest workers, but the leader of the Kurds—an engineer—complained bitterly to me in English about his various problems: the small, hotel room he occupied, the difficulties in getting a good job because he could not travel freely around Europe on the Dutch *laisser-passer* he had been given in lieu of a passport. When I mentioned the plight of the Moroccans, the Kurdish engineer's expression showed the contempt he had for such categories of people. "Well, yes, guest workers," he said. "They chose to come here. I had a villa in Baghdad, and two cars and a swimming pool. I've lost everything."

Meanwhile, one of the Dutchmen in the office was on the telephone, yelling at an immigration official because two other Kurds had been detained at Schiphol Airport to await a hearing that would decide whether they should be given entry. "They're being held in police custody, dammit!" he shouted. "Yes, I know . . . well, put them in an hotel. They won't run away; they've nowhere to go."

When he had hung up, he looked from me to the Kurdish engineer and back again. He gave me a kind of shrug-wink, implying that he knew the engineer was rather a pain in the neck. "But it's not a matter of liking or disliking a person," he said to me in Dutch, echoing the phrase the architect had used. He seemed to realize that I was perplexed by his angry phone conversation. "It's because we no longer want a world in which men in uniforms push around other men in shabby suits," he said. "I wasn't shouting because I'm worried about the comforts of those two Kurds. I *am* worried about their pride as human beings. I *am* worried about the reputation of our city."

The Many Pleasures of Vondel Park

Resting on a bench after a stroll through Vondel Park with their dog, an elderly couple take bemused note of some high-flying activity near by.

"Live and let live" is a maxim that could well have been chosen with Amsterdammers in mind, and nowhere is the easy-going nature of the populace more evident than in Vondel Park, near the city centre. Named for the 17th Century poet Joost van den Vondel, the park contains 120 acres of wooded lawns, paths and ponds that are enjoyed equally by sportsmen and health faddists, pensioners taking their ease and youths letting off steam. At times, certain social groups have assumed dominance there: when the park opened in 1865, for example, it served principally as an after-church promenade for well-to-do families; a century later it became a hippie campground. But no one group can exert a lasting claim on Vondel Park as long as Amsterdammers continue to live by its namesake's wish: "That freedom, like a sun, may shine on all men".

Displaying the fierce concentration of a seasoned angler, an old gentleman sits at his accustomed fishing spot beside one of Vondel Park's lakes, oblivious to a crowd of rock-music enthusiasts gathered to hear a concert.

Four pensioners pass a summer afternoon playing rummy in a secluded, sun-dappled glade that park authorities have thoughtfully furnished with a card table.

On a flower-bordered pathway near the entrance of Vondel Park, women of two generations indulge in a pastime common the world over: admiring a baby.

At the edge of a pond, a yoga student flexes his arm and back muscles . . .

. . . and then flips over into a carefully balanced, jack-knife position.

Turning a lawn in the park into an impromptu stage, a black youth gives Sunday afternoon lessons in modern dance—free to anyone who wishes to join in.

A sodden sheepdog retrieves a branch from a pond near the centre of the park. By-laws restrict Amsterdam's large dog population to leashes in most parts of the city, but in Vondel Park no restraints are imposed, and dogs can exercise to their hearts' content.

2

The Sea Traders

When I first read Mark Twain's description of children in western America lying in bed and counting the whistles of the transcontinental trains going by in the night, I immediately thought back to myself as a little boy in Amsterdam listening to the ships' sirens in the harbour. What the prairies of the American West were to those youngsters, the sea was to us: an immense, romantic realm vibrant with the promise of unknown adventures. It was the backdrop to our daily lives. Our conversation was crammed with nautical expressions and images. To fall on hard times was to "fetch up on a lee shore"; a rich man was said to be "running before the wind"; while someone who was sick or in serious trouble was "lying in front of Pampus", a reference to a notorious shoal just beyond the port. On New Year's Eve we listened with rapture to long lists of ships' names read out on the radio, with season's greetings to and from their crews. And when a harsh wind blew through the streets as I was being tucked into bed, my mother would invariably murmur sympathetically about "the poor sailors".

To a small boy, the sea was a magical place where heroic figures from the past—buccaneers and naval captains—ploughed through the waves in creaking sailing ships. As I grew older, I began to perceive other dimensions of the relationship between Amsterdammers and the sea. At school we were told how the city's rise to prosperity and fame had been linked with sea trade; indeed, the canalside houses of the old town seemed peopled by the ghosts of their original owners: spice merchants, slave traders and ships' captains. At the same time, I came to appreciate how the sea could wreak havoc upon a low-lying city like Amsterdam, which requires an elaborate and costly system of canals, dams, locks and pumps to keep the water in check.

Regardless of how one views it, the sea is "not only a neighbour but a member" of the community, as a 16th-Century writer put it. Before the Second World War, Amsterdammers commonly travelled to some intra-city destinations by boat or ferry. For example, my father's office in Amsterdam was most easily reached by a crude ferry that was hand-winched along a cable stretched across a wide canal. Longer journeys, too, were likely to involve travel over water. If we visited relatives in the northern province of Friesland, we travelled by train as far as the coastal town of Enkhuizen, 25 miles north of Amsterdam, and then took a steamer across the Zuiderzee, the great bay that once linked Amsterdam's old harbour with the North Sea. That was a nasty journey, because the shallowness of the Zuiderzee—nowhere deeper than 10 feet—produced a short and sickening pitch and roll

Sculling his dinghy with sturdy strokes on a single oar, a dock worker ferries himself across Amsterdam's old harbour. The affinity that Amsterdammers have with the sea was summed up by a 17th-Century English writer who noted: "Almost all among them are seamen born and, like frogs, can live on both land and water."

in even the gentlest of winds. I can still smell the lounge on that ship, where travelling salesmen sat drinking glasses of Dutch gin to ward off seasickness.

No steamers ply the Zuiderzee now: about half of it was drained after the Second World War and converted into agricultural land. The area that remains is a freshwater lake called IJsselmeer, of which Amsterdam's old harbour, the IJ (the two letters sound like the English "Y", and stem from a German word meaning "flowing water"), forms one arm. As a child I was fascinated by the harbour, with its bustling activity and exotic smells of coffee, tobacco, tropical hardwoods and other trade goods. I vividly remember the day a friend of my parents, a professional butter taster, took me along as he made an inspection tour of a warehouse on Bickers Island in the western part of the harbour. His equipment consisted of a hollow stick and a paper bag. Occasionally he pointed at random to a butter barrel, which was promptly opened. Dipping his stick deep into the contents, he brought up a sample, tasted it, then spat it into the bag. By this quick and simple procedure, he could grade a consignment of butter for export.

On my latest visit to Amsterdam, I wondered if that same warehouse still stood. Somehow, I doubted it. Since my departure from Amsterdam after the Second World War, the centre of the port's operations had moved several miles farther west, along the North Sea Canal, where the water is deeper and big, automated ships have easy access to the open sea. Nevertheless, I was prompted by nostalgia to visit again the old docks and quays along the IJ—the locus around which Amsterdam grew.

It was a sunny, windy morning when I set foot again on Bickers Island, a long sliver of land artificially created by dumping sand and earth between dock and quays. Until the port's activities shifted, many dock workers lived on Bickers and three other man-made islands—Kattenburg, Wittenburg and Oostenburg—which could be reached only across drawbridges. Their housing, overshadowed by tall, brick warehouses, was badly run down, although the water and sky all around may have taken some of the curse off the narrow little rooms. Most of the islanders were communists, and they were fiercely independent and chauvinistic about their own neighbourhoods. During the German Occupation of 1940-45, these Amsterdammers played a spirited part in the Dutch resistance: appropriately, when a postwar monument was commissioned to commemorate the general strike called by communists to protest against a round-up of Jews in 1941, the symbolic figure of a docker was chosen as the subject.

Now, on my first visit since my schooldays, I found that much of the slum housing had been demolished and replaced by modern factories and warehouses. The navy dockyards were closed and the huge admiralty storehouse had been converted into a maritime museum—one of the best in the world, I learned, but nonetheless devoted to vanished glories. The warehouse I had visited with the butter taster was still there but it stood

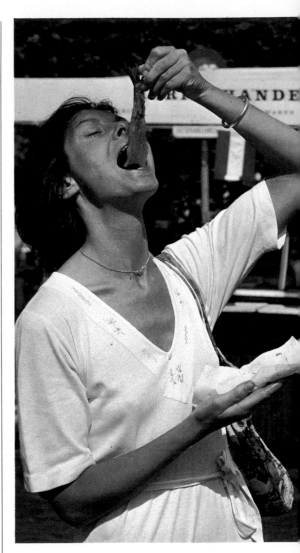

Her head craned back in the approved manner, a visitor to Amsterdam prepares to take a bite from a salted herring purchased at one of the city's open-air snack stalls. Ever since a Dutchman discovered in 1384 that herring could be preserved by salting them in barrels the fish have been a favourite of the local diet—and also a leading export item.

empty, its doors boarded up. Most of the islanders had left and settled elsewhere, and with them had gone much of the neighbourhood spirit.

Walking down streets with names like Tar Gardens and Kipper Hanger —reminders of Amsterdam's long involvement with sailing ships and fishing—I passed a wooden landing stage, overgrown with weeds. A boat service used to call here on its way up the Amstel River to the town of Ouderkerk, a favourite place for excursions 50 years ago. Now, the landing stage was blocked by a decrepit houseboat on which a young woman in jeans and bra was doing her laundry.

Yet the old ambience was not entirely a memory. Some of the narrow streets and the dwellings on them had been repaired and upgraded rather than demolished, and I passed one house that had kept its traditional spy mirror: a small looking-glass attached to the window-frame in such a way that the householder could check the identity of callers without opening the front door, and also keep an eye on the activities of neighbours. Looking into this one from the outside, my eyes met those of an elderly woman ensconced in an easy chair inside, watching the life in the street from her sitting-room. Elsewhere, men were working, just as I remembered, in machine shops under corrugated iron roofs, or on slipways where small boats were being repaired.

From Bickers Island I took a bus past the Central Station, intending to visit Kattenburg Island in the eastern part of the harbour. I missed my stop, however, and ended up on the Surinam Quay, a far outpost of the port. The only other passengers on the bus were two Indonesian ladies. We alighted together at a tall, cast-iron gate that bore the letters K.N.S.M., the initials of a shipping company that started commercial life in the 1850s with services to St. Petersburg and Copenhagen, and that later expanded its routes to South America and the Caribbean. The company offices looked shut, but some work must have been going on, for the two ladies rang a bell and a man in a faded blue uniform shuffled out of a guardhouse to open the gate for them. In the quayside setting, the Indonesian women created an historic tableau: by these very gates, women from the Dutch East Indies used to say goodbye to their native husbands who crewed the Pacific-bound steamers in the 19th Century.

I crossed the street and waited for the bus back to the town centre, my coat flapping in the wind that blew unchecked across the IJ. Flags and pennants were everywhere, even on the railway station farther along the harbour. They reminded me of 17th-Century Dutch naval panoramas; in such paintings, the representations of myriad pennants fluttering made the wind almost palpable. Right here, I reflected, was the confluence of wind and water that fostered Amsterdam's transformation from an obscure little fishing village into a trading city of enormous power and prosperity. But physical conditions favourable to commerce proved no guarantee of enduring success: Amsterdam's maritime heyday lasted barely a century

Herbs and spices shop

Tobacco emporium

Coffee store

Indonesian restaurant

A quartet of Amsterdam businesses, with their proud proprietors in attendance, are redolent reminders of the city's trading heyday when Dutch ships called at colonial ports and settlements from Java to South Africa.

and a half, from the mid-16th Century to the end of the 17th Century. Describing that meteoric rise and abrupt slump, the German traveller Friedrich Carl von Strombeck wrote: "Amsterdam has the form of an immense, ancient theatre, whose stage is the sea. On the programme is the tragi-comedy of the second downfall of Rome. . . ."

The earliest recorded mention of Amsterdam is made in a deed of 1275, issued by the local lord, that granted "the people who live near the Amstel dam" exemption from tolls for the transport of their own goods. A 17th-Century drawing that reconstructed the early settlement shows two lines of houses—one on each side of the Amstel River. The houses were built on dikes that kept the river within its course and that also afforded some protection from storms in the Zuiderzee. A dam, built about 1240 on the site of what is now Dam Square, joined the two banks near the river estuary. Later, behind the dam, the Amstel was diverted into two channels leading to the Zuiderzee; the channels and the river beyond them offered a safe anchorage for fishermen who sailed as far as the English coast to catch great quantities of herring. (There is more than a little truth to the saying that "Amsterdam was built on herring bones".)

By the beginning of the 16th Century, Amsterdam had grown into a walled city with a population of about 12,000. But it was still only one urban centre among many: astonishingly, towards the end of the century nearly half of the country's population were townspeople, mostly engaged in turning the raw materials of foreign lands into finished products for export.

Of all the towns, Amsterdam was in the best position to capture the lion's share of such business, for the reasons given by a Dutchman in the next century: "If any doubt whether Amsterdam be situate as well or better than any other City of Holland for Traffick and Ships let out to Freight, let him but please to consider in how few hours (when the wind is favourable) one may sail from Amsterdam to all the towns of Friesland, Overyssel, Gelderland and North Holland, & vice-versa, seeing there is no alteration of Course or Tides needful."

Making the most of her advantageous position, Amsterdam established a thriving trade with the Baltic countries. The city's ships—each one financed by a co-operative called a *rederij*—sailed to seaports located there to pick up cheap grain that had been raised by serf labour for the Prussian and Polish landowners. They also took on furs and timber (the province of Holland had no forests of its own; and every piece of wood, from the staves of herring casks to the timber piles that propped up Amsterdammers' houses, had to be imported). What Amsterdam itself did not need was transported on to France and Portugal. And on their return voyages, the ships were laden with spices, wine and salt for the northern markets.

Amsterdam's merchant fleet operated in direct competition with vessels of the Hanseatic League, an association of Baltic trading towns. But the

In a peaceful haven off the western part of Amsterdam's old harbour, children dig for worms on a mud bank. Across the water, a solitary training schooner lies berthed where once the pride of the city's sailing fleet tied up.

Dutch shippers soon gained a secure lead over their rivals. For one thing, the German ships could not make the long haul from the Baltic to Iberia and back in a single sailing season; Amsterdam's fleet had no such difficulty, since the city was situated mid-way between the northern and southern markets. For another, the members of the *rederij*, by posting agents in the main markets and running their ships efficiently, could offer lower freight charges than the Germans. As Amsterdam's share of European trade grew, so did the city itself—but not always in desirable fashion. By 1562 the city council was complaining of "slums": 600 houses, inhabited by "unserious folk and riff-raff", built outside the city walls. In the interest of hygiene, the council passed ordinances forbidding the towns-people to throw their slops out of windows.

Remarkably, Amsterdam's boom occurred during the course of an 80-year war with Spain. In 1555, one year before he abdicated to retire to a monastery, the Holy Roman Emperor Charles V handed over to his son, Philip II of Spain, all his Low-Country possessions—17 provinces that, roughly speaking, cover the present-day area of Belgium, Holland and Luxembourg. Philip—unlike his father, who was born in the Belgian city of Ghent and who spoke Dutch—cared only for the greater glory of Spain and the Holy Catholic Church. In 1559 he installed his half-sister Margaret as regent and, after issuing an edict that authorized Inquisitors he appointed to burn, strangle or bury alive unrepentant heretics, he sailed back to Spain.

Philip's repressive measures set off a wave of anti-Catholicism in the Netherlands, where Calvinism, a rigorous form of Protestantism, had attracted many adherents since the publication in 1536 of John Calvin's unorthodox doctrines. The revolt began in Antwerp but spread like wildfire through the Netherlands. In 1566, the year the first public Protestant ser-mon was preached in Amsterdam, mobs of the poor smashed saints' statues and other "popery" in the Oude Kerk, Amsterdam's cathedral. The Dutch nobility at first sided with the established government; but they also rose in arms when it became clear that Philip regarded his possession merely as a vassal state, subject to onerous taxes and tyrannized by the Inquisitors. One of them, William of Orange—Philip's *stadhouder* (lieu-tenant) in Holland—tried to mediate between the Catholic government and the renegades. When that failed, he too went over to the rebels and subsequently became their spokesman and general.

Incensed, Philip dispatched 10,000 soldiers under the Duke of Alva to put down the uprising. So brutally did Alva carry out his master's orders that the pacification became known as the "Spanish Fury". Its principal instrument was a tribunal nicknamed the Council of Blood which could try and condemn at will. William of Orange was an early victim of this wrathful institution. He was outlawed and forced to flee to Germany.

In spite of the paroxysm of rioting in 1566, Amsterdam continued to hedge its bets: the Baltic trade had made the city rich, and it stood to lose a lot if it backed the wrong side. A good proportion of the citizenry greeted Alva as an ally when he marched into Amsterdam in 1573. For a time he had his headquarters in town, living in what is now 113 Warmoesstraat, behind Dam Square. Many Protestants fled or went underground; others, less fortunate, were caught and put to death. Court archives show that a young girl—a near neighbour of Alva's—was executed by being drowned in a barrel for throwing a shoe at a statue in the Oude Kerk.

From Amsterdam, Alva sallied forth to attack the few remaining pockets of resistance. The impending final victory was repeatedly announced in Madrid, but it never came. In October, 1572, William of Orange had returned from exile to be acclaimed as leader of the rebels. The next year, on October 8, William's forces defeated a Spanish army led by Alva's son, and three days later the Spanish fleet was routed on the Zuiderzee. Alva was recalled to Spain in disgrace (he left without paying debts he had run up in Amsterdam), to be replaced by a more conciliatory military governor.

In spite of the turnaround, Amsterdam's religious reformers did not come out into the open until 1578, a year after the Spaniards withdrew from the city. They declared the Protestant faith the official religion, a move euphemistically called the "Alteration"; but instead of executing the Catholics and pro-Spanish collaborators, they simply drove them in carts to a sea-dike east of the town and left them to make their getaway as best they could. Perhaps that was the most praiseworthy act of the city during this rather shabby period. I read the complete story only after I had left school: in my primary school history class, Amsterdam's less-than-universal commitment to the overthrow of tyranny was never mentioned.

Having committed themselves to the Protestant cause, Amsterdammers in 1579 joined other rebels in the northern Netherlands to declare independence from Spain; two years later, the allies founded the Seven

One of the keys to Amsterdam's rise to commercial greatness was the flute, a three-masted vessel developed in the 1590s. Sleek and swift, it was easy to build, could be manned by a relatively small crew, and could carry bulkier cargoes than its foreign rivals.

MARY EVANS PICTURE LIBRARY, LONDON

Islands of Charity

Amsterdam has compiled a shining record of caring for the aged and poor. It began in the 17th Century, when wealthy citizens founded establishments called hofjes—each one actually a clutch of tiny almshouses nestled around a courtyard. Support for the 20 or 30 occupants of such retreats was provided by family trusts, charities, or the city itself. Of the 75 hofjes still in existence, the best-known is the Begijnhof (right), established as a convent in 1346 and converted to its present use after Catholicism was renounced as Holland's official religion. Located just off a shopping thoroughfare, the Begijnhof retains the placid aspect of a village in the very heart of the metropolis.

Two residents of the Begijnhof stroll past a neighbour's rose garden.

Tall buildings and traffic hem in the Begijnhof. At its centre is a former Catholic chapel founded by the Beguine order, from which the hofje takes its name.

BOTH ADAM WOOLFITT, SUSAN GRIGGS AGENCY, LONDON

United Provinces. Thereafter, fortune smiled on the city even more brightly than before; although Spain did not cease its efforts to recoup until 1648.

At the time the rebellion began, Amsterdam had had about 30,000 inhabitants; half-a-century later there were more than a hundred thousand. The rise in population was matched by an expansion of the city's merchant fleet. An Englishman who visited Amsterdam in 1586 wrote: "There belongeth to this town a thousand ships, the least of the number of a hundreth tonne, besides numbers of other ships and lesser vessels." Soon, ships flying the city's flag—three white crosses of St. Andrew on a black and red background—were calling at every port in Europe.

Historians have listed a number of reasons for the boom. The lucrative Baltic trade had led to an accumulation of capital for investment; fuelled by this money, Amsterdam's traditional enterprises of shipbuilding, weaving, dyeing and soap-making evolved from guild crafts into early industries. Calvinism itself fitted hand-in-glove with an early capitalist spirit: according to the new orthodoxy, being rich was a sign of God's grace, provided you worked hard and didn't squander your wealth on sinful luxuries.

I think there was also an intangible, more human, factor involved: the relief of men escaping the yoke of a fanatical overlord found expression in a new spirit of tolerance. In an age when religious bigotry was rife in the world at large, Amsterdam offered citizenship to Catholics, Jews and foreigners. Admittedly they had to pay a fee of eight guilders—equivalent to a Dutch sailor's yearly wage—for the privilege, or else be able to offer a special skill or talent. But there seemed to be no lack of men qualified for the exemption. Merchants who had borrowed new techniques of book-keeping and banking from southern Europe poured into the city. More than a thousand shipwrights won free entry between 1580 and 1604. And Jewish diamond merchants and cutters established workshops in Amsterdam after fleeing Antwerp when that city fell to the Spanish in 1585. A century later, the prevailing atmosphere of tolerance was praised by the famous Amsterdam philosopher Baruch Spinoza, himself the son of an emigré Jewish family. "In this city second to none," he wrote, "men of every nation and sect live together in the utmost harmony." Amsterdam also took pains to protect its citizens when they travelled abroad. Any Amsterdammer anxious about returning to less enlightened countries such as Germany, where so-called witches were still burned at the stake, could buy from the Weigh House on Dam Square a certificate attesting to his metaphysical soundness.

The new mood also encouraged commercial experimentation. Amsterdam merchants began to ask themselves why they should continue to make business transactions in the medium of gold and silver coins, whose real value was reckoned by weight and which were often clipped by unscrupulous traders to about 90 per cent of their face value. Why not use paper money and certificates of deposit instead? All that was needed was a

A Miniature Show House

This four-foot high model of a 17th-Century house—on display at Amsterdam's Rijksmuseum—was created for a family that wanted to memorialize its patrician lifestyle. The model makers carried out their commission in remarkable detail, filling the home with china figurines and furnishing it with miniature Delft wall tiles and crockery.

Sectional view of the entire house

A servant working in the laundry

The stately main bedroom

Master and mistress in the living-room

The tile-decorated kitchen

Tea-time in the dining-room

place of deposit that everyone trusted, and Amsterdam decided to supply such a place. The city opened an exchange bank in 1609, almost a century before London took a similar step, and people started to pay trading debts by simple credit transfers from one account to another, with nothing changing hands but a piece of paper signed by the municipal accountant. Merchants from all over Europe availed themselves of the bank's services. As the economist Adam Smith wrote in his 18th-Century classic, *The Wealth of Nations*, the businessmen knew that, "for every guilder circulated as bank money, there is a correspondent guilder in silver or gold".

But Amsterdammers never lost sight of the fact that the sea, even more than revolutionary trading tactics, was the ultimate key to achieving an economic millennium. Pieter Hooft, a poet born in the city in 1581, made an exhilarating prophecy:

... men of Holland shall outsail and far surpass
All folk, whoe'er they be, that possess ports or roadsteads,
And they shall cleave the blue as Princes of the Sea.
This shall their skill, this their ambition be, to bend
The rearing Ocean to their will; to wrench the bit
Into the mouths of the truculent stubborn winds,
And scorn the sullen roar of billows never plumbed.

First, however, more and better ships were needed. In the late 16th Century, Amsterdam's shipbuilders had come up with a vessel called a flute, a brilliant pelagic creation that was cheap and easy to construct. Four to six times as long as it was wide, with rounded sides that narrowed towards the deck, the flute was speedier than its French and English competitors. It also reduced the tolls exacted by European port authorities, who charged according to the width of deck cargoes. In addition to these virtues, it was manned by half the crew required for a traditional design. Not that sailors were difficult to recruit in Amsterdam: church registers of the early 17th Century show that one in every five bridegrooms was a sailor, even though conditions and discipline aboard ship were appalling (sailors found guilty of homosexuality, for example, would be bound to each other and thrown overboard).

Amsterdam now had the ships, the men and the money to expand its overseas trade. The embargoes imposed on Dutch ships by the Spanish and Portuguese, who were still at war with Holland, gave the city's merchants an added incentive to look for new markets beyond Europe. The seeds of the idea had been planted in 1594, when nine merchants from Holland—along with an Antwerp minister and cartographer named Plancius—organized a partnership bearing the pleasantly romantic title of *Compagnie van Verre* (the Company of Afar). They were after the precious spices of the East Indies, which the Portuguese had regarded as their own preserve ever since Vasco da Gama found a sea route to India in 1497. An exploratory fleet that the company sent to Indonesia in 1595

Seven Centuries Since Amstel Dam

1275	First reference to Amsterdam: Floris V, feudal count of Holland, exempts "the people who live near the Amstel dam" from paying tolls on Dutch waterways
1306	Bishop of Utrecht grants charter recognizing city's limited independence under sheriff and magistrates. Consecration of Oude Kerk, city's oldest church
1452	Great fire destroys much of the town, at that time built chiefly of wood
1489	Holy Roman Emperor Maximilian I of Austria grants Amsterdam right to use imperial crown in its armorial bearings as reward for city's support in power struggle with French
1521	Construction of wooden houses banned to reduce fire risks
1568	Outbreak of Eighty Years War. Most of the Netherlands seeks independence from Spain; but Amsterdam, ruled by Catholic officials, resists Calvinist agitation and remains pro-Spanish
1578	Amsterdam joins fight against Spain after bloodless coup expelling Catholic conservative regents
1579	Rebellious provinces unite under terms of Union of Utrecht, effectively founding Dutch Republic
1588	City archives make first mention of an Amsterdam diamond cutter: Pieter Goos, an immigrant from the Spanish Netherlands
1595-97	Cornelius de Houtman, sea-captain employed by company of Amsterdam merchants, makes successful voyage to East Indies, inaugurating direct Dutch trade with the Orient
1599	Willem Blaeu sets up map-making firm, producing the most accurate globes, charts and atlases of the era
1600	Amsterdam becomes world's most important harbour as home port for more than a thousand ocean-going vessels
1602	Dutch East India Company, with main headquarters in Amsterdam, formed to co-ordinate interests of Dutch companies competing for Eastern trade
1609	City Foreign Exchange Bank established to facilitate international trade. Henry Hudson, Englishman employed by Dutch East India Company, sets sail from Amsterdam; explores river and bay in North America later named for him
1611	Municipal Stock Exchange, designed by Hendrick de Keyser, opens to accommodate increasing volume of financial dealings
1612-25	Concentric ring of canals—Herengracht, Keizersgracht, Prinsengracht—begun and western section of ring completed
1617	First theatre, the Schouwburg, opens
1622	Population reaches 105,000 as immigrants from southern Netherlands are attracted by Amsterdam's prosperity
1631	Westerkerk, tallest church in Holland, completed
1632	Baruch Spinoza, Jewish philosopher, born. Athenaeum (later Municipal University) founded
1639	Rembrandt buys large house at 4-6 Jodenbreestraat, marking the high point of his fortunes
1648	Eighty Years War ends; Spain recognizes independence of Dutch Republic of United Provinces
1648-55	Town Hall, designed by Jacob van Campen, completed
1658-63	Southern and eastern sections of the three concentric canals completed
1669	Rembrandt dies, is buried in the Westerkerk
1671-75	Portuguese Synagogue, designed by Elias Bouman, constructed
1672	Invading armies of France's Louis XIV repulsed when Amsterdammers open dikes to flood land around city
1697	Peter the Great, Czar of Russia, works in Amsterdam shipyard to learn Dutch skills

returned to Amsterdam two years later with a surprise cargo of spices and nuts that paid the cost of the voyage but made no profit. To be sure, the enterprise had encountered serious problems: of the four ships and 249 men that originally left Amsterdam, three ships and only 89 men returned. The other ship sank with all hands, and malnutrition or disease accounted for additional loss of life. A second voyage fared better; "only" 85 of a total complement of 550 men on four vessels died from shipboard maladies and accidents. In July, 1599, the four ships, laden with spices, sailed back up the IJ, to be greeted with pealing bells and the plaudits of officialdom.

A Frenchman who watched the celebration wrote: "The Portuguese are in danger of not enjoying much longer the riches of the Orient." He was soon proved right. Ships and men were pooled, and in 1602 the Dutch East India Company, called the V.O.C. after its Dutch initials, was formed. The V.O.C. was granted a trading monopoly by the United Provinces for all the world east of the Cape of Good Hope. Later, the rest of the world was blithely assigned as the preserve of another Amsterdam-based enterprise, the West India Company. For capital, the V.O.C. had six-and-a-half million guilders, 60 per cent of which was put up by Amsterdam companies, the rest by companies in other Dutch towns. It was a staggering amount, possibly equal to half of all the money in circulation in France at that time, but the merchants were so confident of a good return on their investment that they raised their share of the capital in less than a month.

If Amsterdam, by virtue of its wealth and prestige, was in effect the state of Holland, the V.O.C. was a state within a state, with a charter that empowered it to sign treaties with other countries, wage defensive wars and build fortresses. Control of the company was in the hands of the so-called Seventeen Gentlemen, a group of directors elected by the Dutch towns that had financed the enterprise. Amsterdam was represented by eight directors; another eight seats went to the other participating towns, which took turns to elect the seventeenth member, thus preventing Amsterdam from having too powerful a say in the company's affairs. The Gentlemen built the V.O.C. into the largest trading organization the world had seen, with strongholds, plantations and warehouses not only in the East Indies, but also in Ceylon, India, Japan, the Cape of Good Hope and the Persian Gulf. Their West Indies counterparts set up trading outposts in the Caribbean, the provinces of Pernambuco and Bahia in Brazil, and in New Amsterdam—the future New York. New Amsterdam, part of the Dutch territory of New Netherland, was lost to Britain in 1664 and, although it was reconquered in 1673 by 23 ships from Amsterdam—a little-known action —it was handed back to England six months later in exchange for the slave plantations of Surinam, on the coast of South America.

From all corners of the globe, swarms of cargo-laden flutes converged on Amsterdam, which rapidly became the central market of the Western world. Until the V.O.C. was founded, each European port handled only a limited

Signposts in Stone

After a fire destroyed much of the centre of Amsterdam in 1452, the populace adopted a novel device for making their rebuilt homes and businesses easy to locate. The solution was the gable stone, or *gevelsteen*—a rect-angular plaque bearing a bas-relief scene or emblem that symbolized the occupant's name or profession. Often painted in bright colours and placed either high up in a gable or just above a doorway, these identifying plaques drew inspiration from many sources.

Of the examples illustrated here, a beacon in the old harbour (first vertical row) probably represented a harbour pilot or member of the coastguard, while a chiselled depiction of a castle in Malaga, where traders sailed to buy sherry (third row, second from bottom), made a fitting advertisement for a wine mer-chant. Other occupational subjects include two blacksmiths at a forge (second row, sec-ond from bottom), a grass mower wielding a scythe (fifth row, top). Some of the stones are difficult to decipher today: a hooded falcon (fifth row, bottom) may have been the mark of a merchant who dealt in hunting hawks; or it may simply have alluded to the house-owner's surname, like the rather fanciful panther (fourth row, second from top).

The use of gable stones died out in the 18th Century, when the French introduced logic to the address system in the form of house-numbering. Many of the stones dis-appeared when old façades were replaced, and only about 900 such signs now survive in Amsterdam to remind passers-by of a delightful by-way of Dutch artistic invention.

number of commodities, and prices were determined by more or less arbitrary encounters of goods and money. A keg of pepper might cost twice as much in Lisbon as in Genoa; the Baltic ports might be without salt while La Rochelle had a surplus no one wanted to buy. But with the constant flow of goods of every kind to Amsterdam, prices became standardized, making it worthwhile for traders from all over Europe to come to the city to buy or sell. The Amsterdammers themselves were particularly deft deal-makers. In one instance, canny traders made a killing by contracting in advance for all the mace, a spice from Java, that could be produced in five years, then storing the product and selling when the price was high. The Amsterdammers' conspiratorial and cut-throat buying methods became notorious throughout the world.

Whether by fair tactics or foul, the V.O.C. brought in stupendous profits. The company issued shares, something almost unknown then, and during the two centuries of its existence, paid out an average annual dividend of 18 per cent. In the fattest years, the dividends reached 50 per cent or more of the shares' face value.

I interrupted my journey back to the town centre in order to see the former headquarters of the V.O.C., which stands on the corner of Oude Hoogstraat and the Kloveniersburgwal. Built in the 1550s and intended to serve as an arsenal, it is now used by the University of Amsterdam and government officials. There is little about the building to suggest that, three centuries ago, barges carrying ships' cargoes berthed in the canal directly opposite before unloading. Behind its elegant façade, which is decorated with bell-shaped curves, oxen were slaughtered and their carcasses sent to the ships as provisions. On the ground floor, bacon, peas, barley, gin and other victuals for the crews were stored, while on the floors above rested what an old V.O.C. inventory calls "fine Indian wares of nutmeg, cloves, mace, cinnamon and pepper", as well as "linens, silks, fluids, gums, dyes, porcelain and all other merchandise". The men who ran the company were not put off by the mooing oxen and the various smells. To the contrary, they held their meetings on the second floor, directly above the main entrance, although an array of paintings from the Far East lent a measure of aesthetic splendour to their board room.

In near-by buildings were mustered the mercenaries whom the V.O.C. sent out to protect its trading posts. Once the men had signed up, they were usually kept under lock and key lest they desert; and when they were marched out to the ships, they might pass a few of their colleagues swinging on gallows—the price of acting on second thoughts about service in the far corners of the world. As for the natives living in areas under the V.O.C.'s control, they became virtual slaves. The founders of the company had proclaimed an intention to engage in "peaceful and friendly trade", and for their motto they had chosen "Plough up the Sea"—fine words for a land-

Two canvasses of early Amsterdam civic guard companies dwarf an attendant standing in a gallery leading to the city's Historical Museum. Both group portraits were painted when Amsterdam was entering its mercantile prime —the top work by Jacob Lyon in 1628, the bottom one by Thomas de Keyser in 1633.

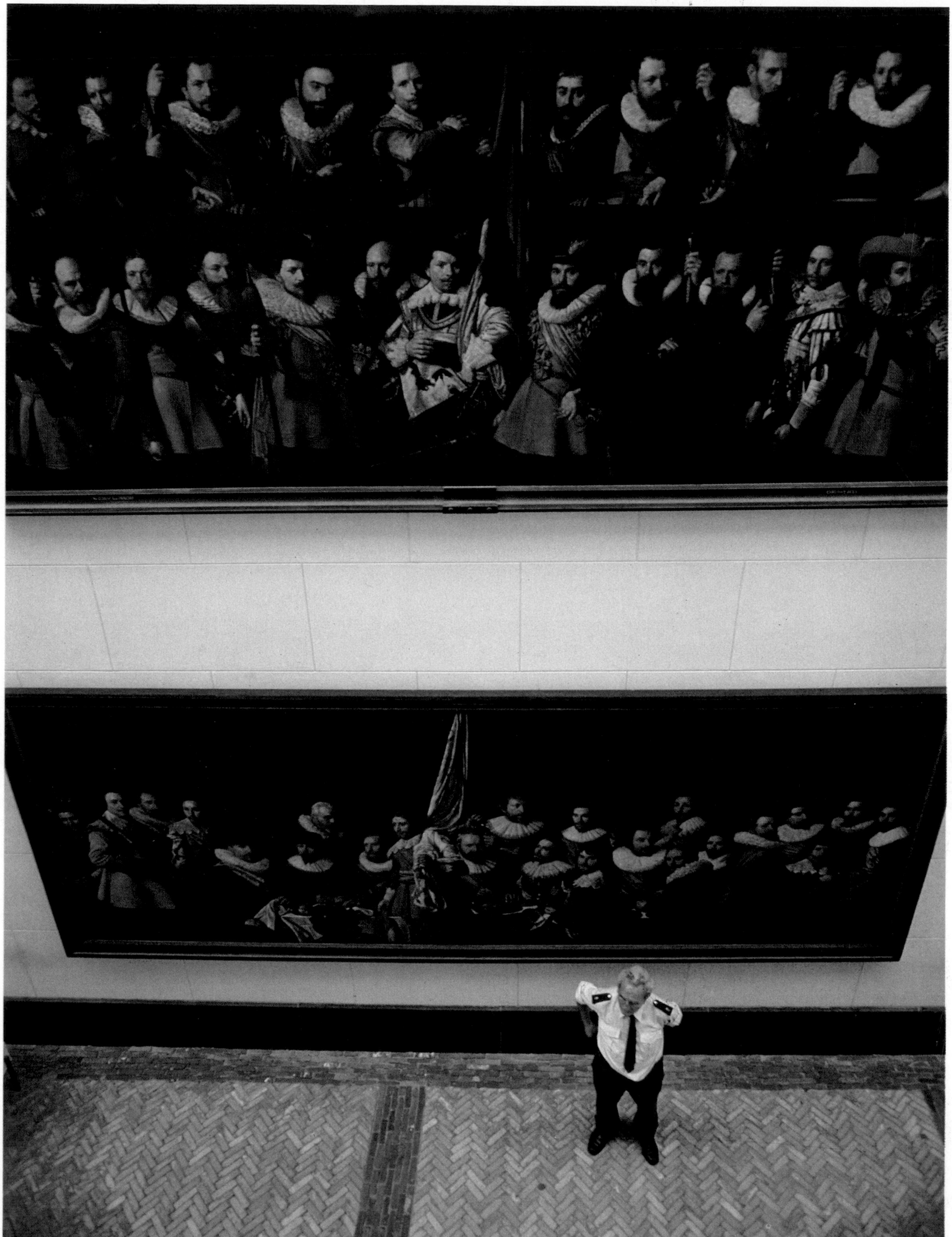

poor country. But the greed of the merchants led them into conflicts with competing European ships and with recalcitrant native populations. "There is nothing in the world that gives one a better right than power and force added to right," wrote one of the Seventeen Gentlemen in 1617. In the 1620s his mailed-fist philosophy was put into practice in the Banda Islands between Borneo and New Guinea; the entire population was either massacred or sold into slavery. A Chinese chronicler, summing up the V.O.C. men whom he met, wrote: "They are covetous and cunning, are very knowledgeable concerning valuable merchandise, and are very clever in the pursuit of gain."

Luckily perhaps for present-day Amsterdammers' peace of mind, the spectacular colonial adventure was never the most important one for the city. In 1666 about three-quarters of Amsterdam's capital was still tied up in the "Mother Commerce", as the Baltic trade was called; most of it involved grain, which remained "the source and root of the most notable commerce and navigation of these lands". At the same time, Amsterdam timber merchants were buying entire forests in Baltic lands to meet the insatiable demand for ships for both the city's own fleet and those of other countries. "Our shipbuilders are invited to England, Germany, Denmark and Sweden—and even to the countries of the enemy," a V.O.C. official complained. He thought the shipbuilders should be constructing more Dutch vessels for the Indies trade.

Amsterdam's spectacular rise was halted in the late 17th Century. English and French politicians and bankers broke the city's trading monopoly by the simple expedient of passing laws that forced their own merchants to use domestic ships. Whereas, in 1650, Holland had about 16,000 vessels on the high seas, more than three times as many as their English rivals, by 1744 the Governor-General of the V.O.C. was complaining: "I am afraid to say how things are with us, for it is shameful. . . . Everything is lacking, good ships, men, officers; and thus one of the principal props of the Netherlands' power is trembling in the balance."

On the high seas, English naval power grew: "The English are about to attack a mountain of gold," a Dutchman wrote with justified foreboding prior to the first Anglo-Dutch war of 1652-54. Trade in the Baltic stuttered on—although by the end of the 17th Century some of the Baltic-bound ships that flew the flag of Amsterdam were, in fact, owned by foreign merchants capitalizing on the city's former reputation. Their skippers boasted openly that, for a few guilders, they could bribe an Amsterdam burgher to give them Dutch ships' papers. The V.O.C. drifted on under its own momentum as a bureaucratic monopoly until it was formally dissolved in 1799, five years after Napoleon's troops invaded Holland with the support of most of the Dutch citizenry.

Amsterdam's gentlemen merchants did not suffer too much from the

NEW YORK PUBLIC LIBRARY

This engraving—the frontispiece of a history of Amsterdam that was first published in 1663—allegorizes the city's prosperous trading empire. Amsterdam is personified as a queen (left) who graciously receives gifts from figures representing the four continents to which her fleet of merchant vessels then sailed.

loss of the great Dutch trading firm. Trimming their sails to the wind, they had started shifting from trade to high finance even before the demise of the V.O.C., for they had realized that in the market-place of money, one man can make as much as a merchant fleet. But for the sailors and ships' carpenters, there were lean times ahead. Their fortunes touched bottom in the winter of 1813-1814, during a continental blockade ordered by Napoleon in the hope of starving his English enemy into submission. That winter, only one ship entered Amsterdam harbour; vessels rotted at their moorings and grass grew on the docks and quays.

Holland recovered its independence in 1813 but while it was building up its trade again, the age of sail was drawing to a close. The new steamers could not negotiate the shallow Zuiderzee, and not until the North Sea Canal was constructed in 1876 did Amsterdam recover from the doldrums. The waterway, now nearly 300 yards wide and 10 miles long, was a lifeline that enabled deep-water ships to reach Amsterdam from the open sea, offering the city a belated chance to join the Industrial Revolution. Recovery was slow, but by the mid-1970s Amsterdam's port was the 14th largest in Europe, employing one in eight of the working population.

Before I left the harbour area, I went to look again at a building that, for me, symbolizes the special affection that Amsterdammers have for sailors— merchant or navy, drunk or sober. It is a round, squat tower on a corner of the harbour basin and Prins Hendriks Quay. Its name, the Schreierstoren, is popularly believed to mean the Weeping Tower. In fact, "Schreiers" stems from a word meaning corner; but every Amsterdam schoolchild knows that this was the place where tearful sailors' wives and sweethearts came to stand on the platform behind the crenellated walls, to wave and stare until the ships vanished into the haze on the horizon.

You can see the tower in the enormous paintings of Amsterdam harbour that Willem van de Velde and his son did in the 17th Century and that now hang in the city's museums. In the paintings it appears dark and low amid the tall masts and triumphant flags, a monument to all the Amsterdammers who fought their way around the Cape of Good Hope against gales, rode out Atlantic storms by manning pumps for days on end, or came to grief while probing wild shores on the other side of the world. These men risked their lives to bring back spices they would never taste and silks they would never wear, while each evening at home, when the setting sun lit up the eastern approaches to the harbour, their families gathered at the tower, hoping to catch a glimpse of a ship that might never return.

3

Outwitting the Waters

The core of Amsterdam has received more artistic homage over a longer period than almost any place on earth. Amsterdammers of the 17th Century were so proud of their city (and of themselves, no doubt) that they surrounded themselves with paintings of their homes, their churches and their harbour. Even the poorer citizens indulged their love of local scenes: "blacksmiths, cobblers, etc., will have some picture or other by their forge and in their stall," wrote an English visitor in 1640. With demand so high, Amsterdam in its glory years supported more painters than any other European city—more than Florence, even. And most of these artists drew particular inspiration from the new town growing outwards from its medieval beginnings—the community of stately houses balanced by their shifting reflections in the canals, the formal lines of gables softened by avenues of linden and elm trees, the church towers that soared heavenwards from the low-lying city.

Even when Amsterdam's fortunes declined, the fashion for townscapes persisted, reaching a peak in 1760 when an art dealer, Pierre Fouquet, commissioned every conceivable town view, which he then had transferred to plates and printed. Not until the end of the 19th Century did painters begin to lose interest in such seemingly simple registrations of reality: George Breitner, whose portraits of a dark, windswept Amsterdam hang in the city's Stedelijk Museum, was perhaps the last of the line. But by then, men working in new media had begun using the city as a model. One was a designer, Willem Wenckebach, who sketched more than 200 views that appeared as engravings in a popular newspaper of the early 1900s; another was a pioneer photographer, Jacob Olie. From 1860 to the turn of the century, Olie lugged a heavy plate camera, tripod and bottles of chemicals through the streets of central Amsterdam. With this primitive equipment he amassed 5,000 pictures of the city.

To me, one of the surprising things about the various kinds of images— 17th-Century paintings, 18th-Century etchings, 19th-Century photographs, and 20th-Century sketches—is that the paintings and drawings match my own concept of the city's core more closely than the camera views. Olie could take pictures only in bright sunlight, and his images show cloudless, colourless skies and white streets with hard shadows. But when I visualize Amsterdam, I see dark clouds, gleaming wet cobblestones, and street lamps mirrored in the waterways—the way some painters saw the city and the way Wenckebach often sketched it. Admittedly, Wenckebach used a little bit of journalistic licence: he copied some scenes from picture

Ripples on the reflective surface of a canal in the heart of old Amsterdam gently distort the images of narrow houses. In a tranquil scene that has changed little in more than 300 years, rooftop television aerials are the only visible trappings of the 20th Century.

postcards (did his editor know, I wonder?); but he improved on composition and, above all, he added the Amsterdam weather.

The other striking thing about the succession of townscapes is how little 17th-Century Amsterdam has changed. Of course, there are no automobiles to be seen in the early views: the streets and quays depicted by the artists breathe a vanished sense of peace, with people walking and holding conversations in the road, little girls in wide hats playing with hoops, and carts being pulled along by horses and dogs (milkmen used dog-carts until about 1930). But automobiles have had only a superficial effect on the appearance of the city centre: you have only to think away the traffic and its sediment of parked vehicles to see that the essence of Amsterdam, the overall feeling, is still there.

That retention of the city's essence came about accidentally, as one consequence of Amsterdam's economic regression during the 18th and 19th Centuries. While other cities were tearing down old buildings and fiercely modernizing, Amsterdam's century-long economic slump carried it through the Industrial Revolution in more or less one piece. (I realize that this was a mixed blessing; no doubt the unemployed would have preferred new factories to venerable churches and bridges.) By the time Amsterdam caught up with the industrial age, an appreciation of old things and traditions had already grown. Opinion is now very much on the side of the conservationists. There are so many committees and action groups hovering protectively over the old buildings that they almost outnumber the guardian angels of yore, of whom medieval philosophers argued that one hundred could stand on the point of a pin.

Due largely to the efforts of conservation groups, Amsterdam has more than 7,000 registered constructions—more monuments to the past than any other city of comparable size can boast. Once something has been so registered with the Ministry of Cultural Affairs, Recreation and Social Welfare, no one can alter its outward appearance. Qualification for preservation does not require architectural beauty: in fact, many of the monuments are warehouses and bridges; and some are not buildings at all, but canals, avenues of trees, or even whole city vistas. But their very multiplicity lends special meaning to the official designation. What makes Amsterdam unique among European cities is that the 7,000 monuments —most of them located in a half-circle little more than half a mile across— are all components of a single, huge Monument: each façade and bridge is a cherished part of the inner-city totality.

In its harmonious blend of stone, wood and water, the old part of the city is an amazingly lovely municipal creation. It becomes even more impressive when one considers that it was built in less than a century and that it has survived in spite of wars, sieges, aerial bombardments, attacks by real-estate promoters and—not the least of its perils—the fact that it rests on mud and sand where digging a three-foot hole will draw water.

COLLECTION AMSTERDAM HISTORICAL MUSEUM

Dam Square in 1656, painted by Johannes Lingelbach, seethes with activity during the building of the Town Hall (left), later to become the Royal Palace.

Surprisingly, much of the credit for the beauty of the townscape goes to the merchants and burghers who sat on Amsterdam's Municipal Council at the end of the 16th Century. These men set aside 1,336 acres for development outside the crowded medieval town and sketched the broad design of a new city. They were motivated less by aesthetic considerations than by Amsterdam's need to adapt to its recently acquired status as a mercantile paradise. They wanted to provide housing for the merchants, craftsmen and refugees pouring into the booming city, build a showpiece that would reflect Amsterdam's commercial greatness and, most important of all, create ideal conditions for trade by sea. Although some work on the new development—notably the construction of canals—had been started as early as the 1550s, it was not until 1609 that the final plan was formally approved, the land for development purchased, and work on the metro-politan expansion begun. Fifty years later most of the construction was finished, and Amsterdam's population had grown from 60,000 to about 200,000—more than the population of 17th-Century Rome or Moscow.

The plan was drawn up by four Amsterdammers: Frans Oetgens, an ex-mayor; Henrik Staets, the city's master carpenter, who had special responsibility for the construction of canals; Lucas Sinck, a surveyor; and Daniel Stalpaert, a surveyor and architect, who was entrusted with the implementation of the overall building programme. There was no existing city that the four men could use as a model, not even Venice—that other notable sea-trading community. Although in guidebooks and on con-ducted tours, Amsterdam is often called the "Venice of the North", this comparison is unjust to the especial beauty of Venice—and also unfair to the remarkable common sense of Oetgens, Staets, Sinck and Stalpaert. Venice is, and was, a city difficult to get around in: when you are on foot, you want for a boat; and when you are afloat, you soon have need to walk. Amsterdam, on the other hand, was designed to allow movement to any part of town either by foot or by boat.

Thus came into being the city's cobweb pattern of waterways—three broad semicircular canals intersected by narrower radial canals. Altogether, more than 600 canals—twice as many as there are in Venice—were dug in an area of less than 2,000 acres. Amsterdam's crowning glory was its concentric arrangement of the three principal canals: the Herengracht, named for the gentlemen who held the power in the city; the Keizers-gracht, named in honour of the Holy Roman Emperor Maximilian I, who in 1489 bestowed a symbolic crown on Amsterdam "since it is not adorned with a coat of arms such as it ought to have"; and the Prinsengracht, named to commemorate William, Prince of Orange, who led the Dutch rebellion against the Spanish. The previous outermost canal, the Singel, which girdled the medieval city, was officially renamed the Koningsgracht (King's Canal); but the citizens of the young republic must have felt that this was pushing royalist sentiment too far because they continued to call it by its original title.

First of the three canals to be started was the Herengracht, part of which had been excavated in 1585 as a defensive moat against the Spanish. Work on the Keizersgracht was begun in 1612 and on the Prinsengracht in 1622. By 1625, the first stage of construction was finished: the three canals started at the harbour, west of where the Central Station now stands, and ended at the Amstel River, completing an arc of slightly less than 90 degrees. To facilitate barge navigation, the canals were laid out in a series of straight sections, with angular bends. In 1658, when the area of the city enclosed by the canals had been built up, the waterways were extended to their present termini near the zoo in Amsterdam East. They were all completed by 1663.

All told, it was an amazing engineering feat. The waterways were dug entirely by pick-and-shovel workers (the word *gracht* comes from a Dutch verb meaning "to dig") who often had to work up to their waists in muddy water. Fortunately, there was no shortage of labour in 17th-Century Amsterdam; the influx of refugees from Spanish-occupied cities provided a cheap and unfailing supply. When the canals had been excavated to a depth of about six feet, their banks were lined with bricks.

One of the trickiest problems the planners had to resolve was how to maintain a constant water level in the canal system while allowing the natural flow of the tides to wash out the waterways and thus keep the city sanitary. The solution was an intricate array of locks that could be closed to prevent the city from flooding when high tides raised the level of the harbour, and that could be opened at low tides to allow stagnant water to drain away into the harbour. So accurately did Staets gauge the correct balance between tides, rainfall and drainage that his blueprint for the system proved effective until 1876, when a dam was thrown across the mouth of the harbour to prevent it from silting up with mud carried in from the Zuiderzee. Because the flow of tidal water was checked by this dam, the water in the canals became stagnant. A bacterial explosion ensued and the tiny organisms turned the turbid water bright red, as if a Biblical plague had struck Amsterdam. The problem was subsequently overcome by building sluices into the dam, which allowed seawater to pour into the harbour from the Zuiderzee and thus cleanse the city's innards.

This continued until 1932, when the Zuiderzee was cut off from the open sea by a dam constructed across its mouth. (Most of the land behind the dam was drained and subsequently reclaimed for agriculture.) Because tidal water no longer reached the city, Amsterdam had to be purged by artificial means. Now, each night, the city gets a seven-hour enema as four million cubic gallons of clean water are pumped into the canals from the IJsselmeer, a freshwater lake that is all that remains of the Zuiderzee. The water is forced westwards through the city and into the North Sea Canal,

Seen from the spire of the Westerkerk, the church where Rembrandt lies buried, houses along the Prinsengracht fan out in a dizzying display of perspective. The 17th-Century merchants for whom these residences were built sacrificed elbow room for canal frontage, but they partly redressed the loss by making the houses taller and deeper than most.

where it is pumped into the North Sea. This massive daily operation earned Amsterdam the sobriquet, "The most beautiful W.C. in the world."

Although the canal system was the focus of the city planners' efforts, the needs of pedestrians and land-traffic were not neglected. As the gangs of labourers dug the canals, teams of carpenters and stonemasons worked behind them, building some 200 bridges to span the waterways. Many of the 17th-Century bridges are still standing and others have been built since, so that today more than a thousand bridges allow pedestrians to move freely about the city (Venice, in spite of the deserved fame of its spans, has a mere 700 or so).

Such a multitude of bridges led to the establishment of a new occupation in 17th-Century Amsterdam: that of *kar-ga-door* (literally cart-go-ahead), whose job was to help haul the carts of traders and street vendors over the hump-backed bridges. *Kar-ga-doors* remained a part of the Amsterdam scene until the introduction of motorized transport made muscle-power unnecessary; in my youth it was a point of honour to lend the cart-haulers a helping hand. I remember the last member of the profession, a little man nicknamed Kikkie, whom I used to see (always dressed in a black sailcloth cap) stationed on the Prinsensluis, the bridge that carries Prinsenstraat across the Prinsengracht. Kikkie's equipment consisted of a length of rope with an iron hook at one end; he fixed the hook to any passing cart that engaged his services. When he died in 1939, he had been a *kar-ga-door* for 50 years.

As the canal network was expanded outwards, earth and clay excavated from the diggings were dumped between the waterways to raise the level of the land on which the new city would be built. On top of the clay base, considerable quantities of sand were spread to provide a well-drained surface. The sand was transported by cart and by barge from the area around Hilversum, east of Amsterdam, and from dunes along the Dutch coast. (The lakes that dot these areas today, originally the pits from which the sand was dug, give some idea of the extent of the operation.)

The land-fill operation created an archipelago of islands—more than 70 main islands, subdivided into hundreds of smaller islets—on which 17th-Century Amsterdam stands. To minimize the risk of flooding, the 1609 plan stipulated that each new island be built up to a height more than two feet above sea level at high tide. Because tides vary in height, later in the century—in 1684—Amsterdam surveyors introduced a standardized system of measuring the height of land relative to sea level. Zero point on the scale was calculated as 10 centimetres above *average* sea level; and Amsterdam's city council ruled that all new building land had to be raised at least 70 centimetres above this base.

Once the land was raised, the Municipal Council divided it into building plots in such a way that 56 per cent of the area of each island was covered

As part of a city-financed renovation of a 17th-Century canalside house, a wooden template is erected to guide the construction of a bell-shaped gable.

STEP GABLE

NECK GABLE

BELL GABLE

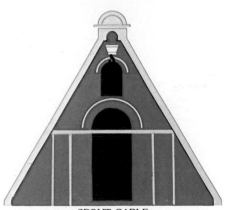

SPOUT GABLE

Rooftop Flourishes

The custom of crowning the narrow houses of old Amsterdam with gables provided an irresistible opportunity for architectural expression. No two gables were precisely alike, although all followed basic patterns. In the 16th Century, gables had steps or spouts that adhered to roof outlines. Later, curving neck or bell gables indicated an Italian influence. By the late 18th Century, gable styles took a final turn—to the clean, conservative lines of the French cornice.

CORNICE

NORMAN BANCROFT-HUNT

by buildings—a much higher percentage than modern planners allow for. When the plots had been marked out, they were sold on the open market—with strict provisos. For example, if the plot was to be used for a private house, the purchaser undertook to use only a type of greenish brick imported from Germany; to install a sanitary privy in the dwelling; and to pay for the cost of maintaining both the footpaths that ran past his land and the sections of canal banks that bordered it.

In addition, before building could commence, the supporting timber piles on which all Amsterdam houses were erected were inspected by municipal surveyors to see if they conformed to standards that had been laid down in 1489. The piles had to be fashioned from tall Scandinavian pines (hardwoods, such as oak, are just as resistant to rot but rarely grow so straight) and sunk in the waterlogged subsoil to a depth of at least 40 feet. Also, because water itself tends to preserve submerged timber, the outer masonry walls of any new building had to be attached to the tops of the piles at points *below* the ground water level. So strictly were these rules followed that most of the underwater piles sunk in the 17th Century—an estimated five million of them—are still solid today.

The council members who drew up the 1609 master plan also introduced a city-wide zoning scheme. Frontages along the harbour, the Brouwersgracht and sections of some other canals were set aside for warehouses. The thoroughfares along the main canals were reserved for the mansions (and, in some cases, warehouses) of wealthy merchants and burghers, while the streets bordering the radial canals were given over to the homes and businesses of craftsmen, artisans and shopkeepers. The eastern sector of the new city, beyond the Amstel, was the farthest from the old city centre and the least desirable. The council had difficulty developing it, so the city gave away many parcels of land to charitable institutions or sold plots at discount prices to immigrants and refugees—many of them Jews from Antwerp and elsewhere.

Amsterdam's poorest citizens—the unskilled labourers, pedlars and the unemployed—ended up in the Jordaan, a medieval district west of the old city walls that the council tried to re-develop between 1612 and the middle of that century. It had always been a slum area, and although the council tried to give the district a facelift by offering 20-foot-square building lots at bargain prices, there were few takers. The inhabitants of the Jordaan remained squatters, who built where they wanted. As Amsterdam's population grew, the district became a maze of narrow streets and alleys lined by small, tumbledown houses: the bottom rung of the economic ladder. Yet, in spite of the abject poverty of most of its inhabitants, it developed a liveliness and sense of community all but unique among Amsterdam's neighbourhoods.

Obviously, the most coveted addresses in the new town were those along the three main canals. The richest citizens settled around the kink in the

Carrying a bargain bought at the local flea market, a resident of a canalside house struggles up the stairs to her top-floor flat. The architects of these narrow houses saved interior space by designing narrow staircases that, like the steep companion ways in old sailing ships, almost have to be scaled.

Herengracht where it now meets Spiegelstraat. This area came to be called the *Bocht*, or Bend; and when I lived in Amsterdam, it was still the city's most exclusive quarter. But any house on the main canals reflected status.

Almost all these canalside dwellings—called *grachtenhuizen*—are surprisingly small compared with what the rich in other countries built for themselves. Not that grandeur was lacking in the repertory of 17th-Century Dutch architects. Justus Vingboons, for example, one of two brothers responsible for designing many of Amsterdam's *grachtenhuizen*, had such a reputation in Europe that he was commissioned to design a palace in Stockholm for the Swedish House of Lords. It was completed in 1656 and has been called the finest building in Sweden. A few great mansions arose in 17th-Century Amsterdam, too, but they were built for a privileged handful or merchant princes, such as the Trip brothers—arms manufacturers, mine owners and traders, who had extensive business dealings with Sweden. Their house, now the Dutch Royal Academy of Sciences, stands on the Kloveniersburgwal, at what is now number 29. Across the canal, almost opposite the stately residence, a tiny house built of the same German sandstone was constructed for the Trips' coachman, who is reputed to have muttered disgustedly, "I wish I had a house as wide as their front door," and who got his wish.

One reason sometimes given for the smallness of the great majority of Amsterdam houses is that the original owners were too mean to lavish large sums of money on grand residences. I won't insist that this explanation doesn't have an element of truth, but it is only part of the story. The pocketbooks of the original merchant occupants were often stretched thin by their far-flung trading ventures: to increase their fortunes, they wanted every penny of profit from the sale of a cargo for investment in more voyages. In any case, there was simply no room for most merchants to indulge any expensive wishes they may have had. Canal frontage was at such a premium that the council initially restricted the width of the houses to 26 feet—enough to accommodate three good-sized windows. (The rule was waived only for such wealthy and influential notables as the Trip brothers.) Later, the rule was relaxed a bit and new houses were permitted to have a width sufficient for five windows. To compensate for their narrowness, most houses reached far back (as much as 180 feet), and gardens 80 feet long were created behind them. Surprisingly, the rear façades were as carefully constructed as those at the front. "Our Lord finished off a canary's behind as neatly as its front," is how one 17th-Century Amsterdam architect described this apparent extravagance.

Most of the *grachtenhuizen* were built four storeys high: the lower three floors were given over to living space, while the top floor was reserved for storing merchandise. From here, goods could be lowered down to the streets, carried across the road to barges moored on the canals, and then floated out to the cargo ships anchored in the IJ. In fact, Amsterdammers considered the untrammelled movements of goods so important that when a council member suggested in the late 16th Century that, instead of building the Keizersgracht, a wide avenue offering fine views be created in its place, his idea was received with the scorn that nowadays would be levelled at a scheme for a shopping centre that didn't include a car park.

To facilitate the hoisting and lowering of goods from the attic warehouses, the builders resorted to a clever tactic: they constructed the front façades of the *grachtenhuizen* with a forward list of as much as five degrees. This tilt not only prevented damage to the brickwork when crates and bales were raised or lowered, it also kept rain out of the open attic windows when goods were being moved. In addition to its practical value, a leaning façade had—and still has—a pleasing aspect to the eye. When you stand in front of such a house and look up, the frontage appears perpendicular, since the forward tilt is offset by the effect of perspective that usually makes the upper part of a building look narrower than its lower part. It is a very neat trick, albeit an unintentional one, but unfortunately the style was abandoned in the 19th Century—probably because the requisite craftsmanship became too expensive. As a result, when you look at a street made up of both leaning houses and conventional, straight-fronted dwellings, the newer houses appear to topple backwards compared with their older neighbours—or the older ones appear to lean forward, depending on where you focus your eyes.

Another feature of the *grachtenhuizen* is the hoisting beam set into the gable above the attic window. In other Dutch towns, only warehouses have these beams; but in Amsterdam every old house is so equipped (although the more snobbish owners insisted on hoists that, when not in use, could be rolled inside and hidden behind shutters, like cannons on old warships). Today, these beams are as indispensable as ever. To save living space in the narrow houses, the architects designed staircases that are little more than glorified ladders. They are rarely more than a couple of feet wide and, because they rise from ground floor to attic without any turns, they are so steep that the uninitiated tend to climb them on all fours. You cannot manoeuvre a table, let alone a bed or a piano up the stairs; all large items of furniture have to be raised via the hoist beam and swung in through a window on the floor that is to be furnished. Understandably, moving house in Amsterdam is a laborious and time-consuming affair.

In summing up the appearance of the *grachtenhuizen*, Gerald Burke, the author of a 20th-Century book on Amsterdam's development, said they represented "architectural good manners". It is true that the strictly symmetrical design and lack of ostentatious ornamentation suggest a restrained and refined approach; Amsterdammers themselves call the houses *deftig*, a word that connotes dignity, respectability and stateliness. But they also have another aspect, which I first saw described by

Moving In by Moving Up

Because staircases in the old town are narrow and pitched at a dauntingly steep angle, furniture and other bulky goods must be moved in through windows. To make the job easier, each canalside dwelling is fitted with a heavy wooden hoist beam that runs the length of the roof and protrudes a few feet beyond the gable. At the end of the beam is an iron hook that can be equipped with a block and tackle for heavy haulage.

The slight forward tilt of the older façades ensures that goods hang clear as they are raised. And wide windows on all floors—some of them with detachable frames—give access to practically any item of furniture a home-owner might desire, including the traditional bane of removal men: a piano.

Protected by a tarpaulin, a piano is pulled through the window one floor below a rigged hoist beam.

While a friend on the pavement far below steadies the pulley rope, two removers (left) reach out for a cane-bottomed chair. Since hauling furniture through the air is a perilous procedure by nature, a pair of helpers supervise the operation at the gable window (above), monitoring the hoist and keeping an eye on the block and tackle.

Sacheverell Sitwell, the English poet and essayist, who visited Holland in 1946 and wrote a lyrical and insightful book about his travels. Comparing 17th-Century Amsterdam houses with those in London, Sitwell advanced the opinion that the little flourishes that embellish Amsterdam houses—decorative gables, stucco-enriched hallways, painted interior wall panels—show an unexpected "delight in living".

The most salient expression of this architectural *joie de vivre* are the gables that top each façade. An 18th-Century map illustrates every single *grachtenhuis* in relief and shows that each one is embellished with a different pattern of gable. Architects classify the various types as ornithologists do birds: there are stepped, pilaster, neck, curved-neck, bottle, and corniche gable styles; but no two are identical in all details. (The basic types of Amsterdam gables appear on page 63.)

On some older houses the gables bear bas-relief plaques that served the purpose of modern house numbers: these little works variously represented the occupation of the owner, or his place of birth, or some important event in his life. They might be based on a joke or riddle, or on a Biblical scene or simply on some flight of fancy. The impulse of Amsterdammers to embroider the basic design of their houses did not stop there. Well-to-do owners decorated the brickwork of their façades with fanciful sculptures: one of the best-known, on the façade of a mansion on Herengracht, is of St. Michael standing astride a slain dragon. The sculpture rests on a plinth fashioned in the shape of an elephant's head. Even the functional hoisting beams were often given decorative treatment. Many were shaped into grimacing gargoyles or ships' prows; the mechanism of a beam on a house in Prins Hendrikkade is concealed in a representation of a lion's head.

I find Sitwell's "delight in living" evident in the overall pattern of the houses as well as in their individual details. This is due largely to their proximity to water. The canals are an integral part of the pattern—soothing and softening the rows of houses on either bank by creating a complex interplay of reflections. The houses seem perfectly designed to take advantage of the mirror that lies between them: because they are so narrow, their images don't break up on the water's surface; although the reflections ripple, each remains recognizably one house. The waterways also lend an element of security to one's overall impression of the centre of Amsterdam. I could never feel lost in a town built on a river or by the sea: the tie with the rest of the world is there. Amsterdam's houses appear almost animistically aware of this tie. They neither huddle nor strut; instead, they stand tall and serene at the start of the sea-road to the ends of the earth. And for the traders who built the houses, there was the added comfort of seeing water—their potential enemy—safely embanked.

All this, I'm sure, was not in the minds of the city architects or their customers. I admit that most of these were money-counting Protestants.

In a city famed for its narrow houses, two addresses have particular credentials for attention. The dwelling above, number 26 Kloveniersburgwal, was originally tenanted by a coachman whose modest wish for a home only as wide as his master's front door was granted. Tour guides sometimes describe No. 7 Singel (opposite) as the narrowest house in Amsterdam; in fact, it is not a residence but a façade built to close off an alleyway.

Moving In by Moving Up

Because staircases in the old town are narrow and pitched at a dauntingly steep angle, furniture and other bulky goods must be moved in through windows. To make the job easier, each canalside dwelling is fitted with a heavy wooden hoist beam that runs the length of the roof and protrudes a few feet beyond the gable. At the end of the beam is an iron hook that can be equipped with a block and tackle for heavy haulage.

The slight forward tilt of the older façades ensures that goods hang clear as they are raised. And wide windows on all floors—some of them with detachable frames—give access to practically any item of furniture a home-owner might desire, including the traditional bane of removal men: a piano.

Protected by a tarpaulin, a piano is pulled through the window one floor below a rigged hoist beam.

While a friend on the pavement far below
steadies the pulley rope, two removers
(left) reach out for a cane-bottomed chair.
Since hauling furniture through the air is
a perilous procedure by nature, a pair of
helpers supervise the operation at the gable
window (above), monitoring the hoist and
keeping an eye on the block and tackle.

Sacheverell Sitwell, the English poet and essayist, who visited Holland in 1946 and wrote a lyrical and insightful book about his travels. Comparing 17th-Century Amsterdam houses with those in London, Sitwell advanced the opinion that the little flourishes that embellish Amsterdam houses—decorative gables, stucco-enriched hallways, painted interior wall panels—show an unexpected "delight in living".

The most salient expression of this architectural *joie de vivre* are the gables that top each façade. An 18th-Century map illustrates every single *grachtenhuis* in relief and shows that each one is embellished with a different pattern of gable. Architects classify the various types as ornithologists do birds: there are stepped, pilaster, neck, curved-neck, bottle, and corniche gable styles; but no two are identical in all details. (The basic types of Amsterdam gables appear on page 63.)

On some older houses the gables bear bas-relief plaques that served the purpose of modern house numbers: these little works variously represented the occupation of the owner, or his place of birth, or some important event in his life. They might be based on a joke or riddle, or on a Biblical scene or simply on some flight of fancy. The impulse of Amsterdammers to embroider the basic design of their houses did not stop there. Well-to-do owners decorated the brickwork of their façades with fanciful sculptures: one of the best-known, on the façade of a mansion on Herengracht, is of St. Michael standing astride a slain dragon. The sculpture rests on a plinth fashioned in the shape of an elephant's head. Even the functional hoisting beams were often given decorative treatment. Many were shaped into grimacing gargoyles or ships' prows; the mechanism of a beam on a house in Prins Hendrikkade is concealed in a representation of a lion's head.

I find Sitwell's "delight in living" evident in the overall pattern of the houses as well as in their individual details. This is due largely to their proximity to water. The canals are an integral part of the pattern—soothing and softening the rows of houses on either bank by creating a complex interplay of reflections. The houses seem perfectly designed to take advantage of the mirror that lies between them: because they are so narrow, their images don't break up on the water's surface; although the reflections ripple, each remains recognizably one house. The waterways also lend an element of security to one's overall impression of the centre of Amsterdam. I could never feel lost in a town built on a river or by the sea: the tie with the rest of the world is there. Amsterdam's houses appear almost animistically aware of this tie. They neither huddle nor strut; instead, they stand tall and serene at the start of the sea-road to the ends of the earth. And for the traders who built the houses, there was the added comfort of seeing water—their potential enemy—safely embanked.

All this, I'm sure, was not in the minds of the city architects or their customers. I admit that most of these were money-counting Protestants.

In a city famed for its narrow houses, two addresses have particular credentials for attention. The dwelling above, number 26 Kloveniersburgwal, was originally tenanted by a coachman whose modest wish for a home only as wide as his master's front door was granted. Tour guides sometimes describe No. 7 Singel (opposite) as the narrowest house in Amsterdam; in fact, it is not a residence but a façade built to close off an alleyway.

But so were the burghers of Geneva, for example, where the dark sad streets bend low as if in fear of hell fire itself. The Amsterdammers of the 17th Century thought that everything was possible; and this attitude, far from dooming them to a narrow materialism, filled them with the joy of being graced by God, of life being good. Inevitably, the mood helped shape their architecture.

Sitwell, like a good poet, did not go in for laborious analyses. He simply wrote what he felt, using words with dazzling economy. I particularly like his characterization of the Westerkerk, Amsterdam's tallest church, which stands near the western section of the Prinsengracht. It was begun in 1620 by Hendrik de Keyser, who died before its completion a year later. The Westerkerk, Sitwell notes, possessed a "fervency" lacking in the London churches for which it subsequently served as a model. Just so, I thought, when I looked again at the church. Here is a building not for polite church-goers but for men and women almost rising from their seats in the bliss of sure salvation. The church itself seems to be straining towards the heavens.

But Sitwell really stole my heart by winding up his essay on Amsterdam with the unhesitant announcement that the esteemed 17th-Century archi-tect Jacob van Campen was too correct for his taste, a bit of a bore—in sum, a man with a heavy and unimaginative hand. An Amsterdammer who professed such an opinion would be guilty of downright *lèse majesté*, for Van Campen owes his reputation to his design of the Royal Palace, originally built to serve as the Town Hall, on Dam Square. This pile, we were taught at school, was the Eighth Wonder of the World. I had never heard anything but praise for it until I read Sitwell, and I was comforted to find an impartial observer who shared my own doubts about the building.

I admit that the palace is very large, and I will concede that it is *deftig*; but what a weight it is, how it looms over the square! To me, the palace represents Amsterdam's power at its apogee—but petrified. It was started in 1648 and completed in 1655 on a foundation of 13,659 piles—a figure drummed into me at school, where we were taught to remember the number by taking the days in a year, and adding a 1 in front and a 9 at the end. The building is not typically Dutch. Instead of using local brick for the construction, the builders imported Irish sandstone (Holland has no native stone). Instead of decorating the façade with a traditional gable, Van Campen made the centrepiece of the building in the form of a vast tympanum—a classically inspired triangular gable—which was decorated with a frieze depicting sea-monsters and allegorical figures paying homage to the Virgin of Peace. The frieze was sculpted by Flemish stonemasons specially commissioned by the council: it was as if the city fathers were embarrassed by the more homespun artistry of their own craftsmen.

Inside the building, the halls and galleries were supported by soaring pillars, paved with marble and hung with ponderously allegorical paintings (one shows figures representing Death and Punishment trampling on

This view along an alley juxtaposes two masterworks by the 17th-Century architect Hendrik de Keyser: the Bartolotti mansion and, behind it, the Westerkerk, Amsterdam's tallest church. On top of the 255-foot church tower is a crown modelled after one granted to the city in 1489 by Maximilian I, first of the Holy Roman Emperors who ruled the Netherlands from 1486 to 1556.

other figures symbolizing Greed and Envy). Such furnishings must have seemed awesome to the ordinary citizens for whom the building was meant to serve as a civic centre. Rembrandt was commissioned to do two paintings for the Town Hall, but the council rejected both. One of his works, a portrait of a Roman consul, ended up in Romania and subsequently disappeared. The other, a study of Batavian tribesmen (ancestors of the Dutch who lived between the Rhine and Meuse Rivers in the 4th Century A.D.) conspiring to overthrow their Roman overlords, was bought by a Swedish family and now hangs—to the regret of present-day Amsterdammers—in Stockholm's National Museum. The reasons for the rejection of the first portrait are not known, but it is likely that the council members were dismayed by the latter work's central figure: Claudius Civilis, a Dutch folk-hero, who was portrayed with tormented features and only one eye. It may seem perverse, but I am glad that the councillors refused Rembrandt's paintings. Without the attraction that they would have given the palace, I can think of no reason why I should want to visit it.

I mentioned previously that the conservationists have won the battle to preserve the old town—for the time being at least—by pressuring the municipality into forbidding any alterations to the exterior walls of registered buildings. But successful preservation requires more than this official "Don't". Amsterdam, with national help, also foots about half the bill for the restoration and upkeep of historic buildings; the property owner pays the rest. When funds are allotted, the authorities attach no conditions limiting the use to which the interior of a renovated building may be put. Many 17th-Century houses have been converted into business premises such as banks or restaurants, others into art galleries or museums. Only the façade must remain unchanged.

A good proportion of the municipal support is earmarked for various foundations that buy dilapidated properties, rebuild them and then rent them out. Private home-owners, too, may receive funds to restore their houses. I know one such beneficiary—a man who bought a house on the Prinsengracht, near the Amstel River, shortly after the Second World War. At the time, that area was rather run-down and the house, which had been a fur-dealer's shop and storeroom, was dark and smelly. He spruced it up, however, and everyone envied him his find until visitors began to notice that their drinks spilled over without anyone touching them. The building was toppling. With the sole stipulation that the façade be restored to its original 300-year-old state, the city offered a large sum towards the cost of rebuilding. The entire job required the equivalent of $100,000 and involved the sinking of new foundations—a year's work in all.

As an inseparable part of the townscape, even Amsterdam's trees qualify for some of the preservation funds. According to the most recent census by the city's parks department, there are 75,000 trees in Amsterdam, most of them planted along the canal banks. Not only was every tree counted individually, but each received a medical check-up. This was necessary because the tightly packed, sandy soil on which Amsterdam stands was constricting the growth of the trees while domestic gas leaking from underground pipes was making some of them sickly.

In addition, in the early 1970s many of the city's elm trees were found to be blighted by a fungal attack called Dutch Elm Disease (so named, incidentally, not because it started in Holland but because the Dutch have studied it more thoroughly than anyone else). Tree doctors now inspect the trees regularly and minister to the unhealthy ones by injecting them with drugs or by amputating diseased limbs. Specimens that are beyond saving are felled and replaced with healthy saplings. Before going on their rounds, these municipally paid specialists study infra-red aerial photographs, commissioned by the city, in which the foliage of healthy trees shows up as bright red, while that of sickly trees shows as pale pink, and that of old trees as very dark red.

Such costly attention to detail may seem an unjustifiable extravagance, yet few Amsterdammers resent the expenditure of public funds for preservation. For one thing, the old city is not a mausoleum for treasures of the past; it is a living community, and the citizens who live, work and play in it are as much a part of the townscape as the counterpoint of water, gables and trees. The credit for that is due to Amsterdam's 17th-Century planners who, by exercising strict control over the building programme, succeeded in creating an environment in which public and private needs were, and are, balanced. But most of all, Amsterdammers understand what their city cost in terms of endeavour. They know that, before a single brick could be laid, the land had to be drained, raised and consolidated. I suspect that even the most fervent Calvinist in Amsterdam is guilty of the sin of Pride when he contemplates the remarkable labours of his ancestors.

A Floating Population

On the top deck of a barge moored along the Brouwersgracht, a young couple and their guest indulge in a little easy living on a cloudy summer afternoon.

Packed bow-to-stern along the waterways of Amsterdam are some 2,500 houseboats—home for a mixed community of artists and artisans, bourgeois and bohemians. Ranging from sleek, chic craft to ramshackle hulks that flout conventional notions of comfort and sanitation, the floating residences were originally welcomed by city authorities as a remedy for the post-Second World War housing shortage. Now, however, a hostile officialdom views the vessels as a source of pollution. New houseboats are refused moorings and cash rewards are offered to owners of dilapidated craft to move to dry land. But boat owners have largely ignored the financial inducements as well as the registration requirements (about half the fleet is illegally moored). For an eccentric minority, petty inconvenience cannot dampen the pleasures of city-living afloat.

For some canal-dwellers, the houseboats are workplaces as well as homes. On this multicoloured barge, a long-haired tailor makes trousers for a living.

ADAM WOOLFITT. SUSAN GRIGGS AGENCY, LONDON

A converted barge, conservatively decorated with lace curtains and potted plants, gets a fresh coat of paint from its mistress.

Two youngsters camp out on a tiny boat lacking the quayside electrical or freshwater hook-ups of most of its neighbours.

As a sightseeing launch glides past the window of their houseboat, members of a theatrical troupe while away the afternoon with a stint on their instruments.

A mother and son enjoy all the comforts of licensed houseboat living—including a panoramic picture-window. The residence was built to their specifications.

While some cats sun themselves and others eat or sleep, a keeper at a charity-supported floating home for feline strays cuddles one of his hundred lodgers.

Unperturbed by the antics of an inquisitive pet, a young musician with do-it-yourself talents tunes one of the two pianos aboard his waterborne studio.

An Amsterdam couple who have spent five years afloat assemble with their two daughters and a solemn-faced doll amid the rich patina of their living-room.

Like a latter-day Noah, a white-bearded American artist cuts a patriarchal figure in the straw-strewn barge he shares with a companion on the Amstel River. Their home is an exercise in elegant primitivism, complete with rough-hewn support posts and a loft over the bed.

A sinking houseboat on Prinsengracht provides a cautionary lesson for would-be barge owners. Its owner overloaded it in an attempt to pass under a low bridge.

4

That Special Trait

Nothing is more dangerous, I suppose, than to try to sum up the individuality of a city in a single word. But if I had to settle for one adjective that distils Amsterdam's peculiar genius, it would be the Dutch word *gezellig*. Attempts at precise translation are likely to spawn a series of near-misses; but in essence, *gezellig* means both cosy and convivial, both intimate and sociable. The blend of these various shades of meaning adds up to an aspect of character that is more pronounced in Amsterdammers than in other inhabitants of Holland—and surely more pronounced than in city dwellers of other lands. If it weren't for Amsterdam, in fact, one might logically assume that big-city life and *gezelligheid*—the noun for this bent of personality and preference—just do not mix.

Gezelligheid is an elusive trait, easily ignored but perhaps more easily exaggerated in the fleeting impressions of foreign visitors, who tend to equate it solely with the easy-going manner of Amsterdammers and their fondness for old-fashioned but snug furnishings: colourful window-boxes, lace curtains, and so on. Such things are undeniable manifestations of the phenomenon. Yet, at the risk of muddying the issue, I think I should start out by saying what *gezelligheid* is *not*.

One must, above all, avoid confusing it with what I call the "Hans Brinker" vision of Holland and Amsterdam. *Hans Brinker; or the Silver Skates*, an enormously popular children's book by the 19th-Century American writer Mary Mapes Dodge, painted a picture of a quaint little society in which friendly but phlegmatic burghers lived out their lives sublimely unaware of the goings-on in the great world outside. I do not know the source of Miss Dodge's ideas (the "Dutch" words in her book are not Dutch at all, but misspelled German); still, it is a charming story, and its powerful hold on generations of readers is not yet broken. The *gezellig* reality differs from that of Miss Dodge in several respects. For one thing, many Amsterdammers are something less than paragons of affability. For another, Amsterdam and Holland, although modest in size, are not by any stretch of the imagination "quaint". To the contrary, while *gezelligheid* is bound up with a love of home, family and friends, it is also rooted in the Amsterdammers' restlessness, their desire to be part of the wide world, with all its infinite possibilities.

I suspect that one side of this trait—the love of home—was born in the early years of the Dutch republic, when a tiny nation of a few million people found itself at odds with the might of Spain. Thrown on their own resources, the Dutch developed a fervent pride in their beleaguered

A bouquet of carnations nestles in a battered but still gleaming tuba hung outside a music shop on Spuistraat. Flowers—fresh-cut or dried, grown in window boxes or cultivated in backyard plots—are an ubiquitous expression of Amsterdammers' taste for cosy surroundings.

country. And yet, even in those troubled days, Amsterdammers were abandoning their homes, wives, children and country to embark on quests to unknown lands in the farthest corners of the globe. Even stay-at-home citizens must have thrilled to the sight of returning ships sailing up the IJ at the end of a two-year voyage; and I like to think that they, too, must have dreamed of following the sea road to the Pacific islands that the sailors described over drinks in the harbour taverns.

This persistent duality was deftly summed up by the 20th-Century French writer Albert Camus, who chose Amsterdam as the setting for his novel *La Chute* (The Fall). "They're double," he wrote. "They're here and they're not here." Noticing that many down-to-earth, middle-class homes were decorated with batik cloths and with leather or cardboard shadow-play puppets from Java and the other islands of the East Indies, he imagined the city's inhabitants "praying to the grimacing gods of Java" and living not only in Europe but on the sea "which leads to Cipango and those isles where men die mad and happy".

In his musings, however, Camus barely touched the surface of *gezelligheid* as it evinces itself in the domestic lives of Amsterdammers. To sample the subtle permutations of the phenomenon, you need only walk, for instance, through the Pijp (Pipe), a 19th-Century neighbourhood between the Singelgracht and Sarphati Park, just outside the charmed circle of Amsterdam canals. These cramped streets are an inheritance from the Industrial Revolution at its most unpleasant, and practically every town-planner in Amsterdam dreams of tearing them down. All that can be said in their favour is that they are *gezellig*. Cheerful yellow-and-white striped awnings shade the windows (not that there is such an abundance of sunlight falling into the narrow thoroughfares). Plants not only decorate but virtually fill up every window, and cats doze behind the glass. Curtains are always open and, from early evening on, the interiors are bathed in the soft light of *schemerlampen*, or twilight lamps—the Dutch term for all table lamps and standard lamps equipped with a cloth or paper shade.

The fact that Amsterdammers do not draw the curtains after dark has been amply commented upon by foreign visitors. I have often seen it ascribed to a Calvinist need to show passers-by that there is nothing to hide, but I don't believe that for one moment. Amsterdam is less Calvinist, in the widest sense of that term, than any other spot in the Netherlands; it has never been a puritanical city. Nor have I ever heard of this practice in other fortresses of Calvinism ("hotbeds" would be an unhappy metaphor) such as Geneva or Basle. I would attribute the open curtains to that same dichotomy maintained before: to be at home and to be out, to be intimate and to long for the company of all the world.

Being *gezellig* has the specific meaning of not holding yourself aloof, of mixing easily and with a minimum of ceremony. In Amsterdam, you can still ring a friend's doorbell without telephoning first to say you are

Riding amid a resplendent cortege, a councilman representing St. Nicholas—the patron of the city—bestows his blessings in a ceremony held in late November.

coming. Moreover, callers, from mailmen to bill collectors, may well be invited into the house for a morning cup of coffee or an afternoon cup of tea.

This sort of casual welcoming is what I best remember about the Saturday mornings of my childhood. The family would gather in the kitchen after the coffee had been made. (Even a woman like my mother, who hated housework, would not have dreamt of doing this in any way other than by grinding beans by hand, putting the grind in a porcelain filter, adding a pinch of salt and a tinier pinch of cocoa, slowly pouring in hot water, and then reheating the resulting coffee extract with milk.) After the coffee was made, the tradesmen began dropping in to collect the weekly bills. They had to climb three flights of stairs to reach our apartment and they might not be paid, for our fortunes fluctuated wildly. But they would always sit down, drink at least one cup of coffee and discuss their problems with my mother, who had a great talent for making people tell her their woes and cheering them up. Those Saturday morning scenes of crowded informality amid the lovely smell of the fresh coffee were veritable orgies of *gezelligheid.*

I do not intend to give Amsterdammers extra points for hospitality. I don't see any reason for assuming that they are more generous than citizens of any other city, and I don't think that they invite each other to parties or dinners more often than people do elsewhere. But the custom of unplanned and unorganized visits throughout the day is indeed special.

The Dutch language also reveals much about Amsterdam society. The cup of coffee sipped by my mother's baker or butcher was a *kopje koffie*; the biscuits served with it were *koekjes.* Those *je* endings are diminutives, and Dutch is full of them. They are simply tacked on to the end of a word: a *kop* is a cup, and a *kopje* is a little cup. But they must not be translated literally: you ask for a *kopje* without in the least expecting a cup smaller than the ordinary size. Some words don't even exist anymore without a diminutive ending; a girl is a *meisje* even if she is six feet tall. This language peculiarity could easily be explained as part of the simple "Hans Brinker" vision of the Dutch. But I would rather attribute the linguistic quirk to *gezelligheid*; it fits my dichotomy: soothing little words used in a broad setting.

Another example that comes to mind may make this point even more clearly. As infants, we were cradled to sleep with a song called *Schuitje-varen* ("Sailing"), which tells of a voyage across the sea in a little boat. What could be more apt? The raw and misty distances of the sea serve to dwarf any boat, yet somehow the gentleness of the words creates a snug, comforting ambience.

In its physical and social manifestations, *gezelligheid* is by no means confined to the home and family, as any evening in Amsterdam will quickly make evident. After dinner, there is an exodus to the cafés, where you can be *gezellig* once more, but with someone else pouring the coffee or the

Spanning the Reguliersgracht at measured intervals, five bridges appear almost to be stacked on top of one another. The canal-laced city boasts more than a thousand bridges, which range from simple masonry structures, as here, to massive, electrically-operated drawbridges.

genever—Dutch gin that is sipped, uniced and unmixed, from little glasses. In a sense, the change of scene is minimal: the cafés often bear a marked resemblance to Amsterdam living-rooms, with old prints or paintings on the walls, and sometimes carpets on the tables instead of cloths. Most of the cafés are family concerns.

This sort of cosiness in public places is relatively new. During its commercial heyday, Amsterdam, like virtually all other cities, had its taverns for the people and its coffee houses and clubs for gentlemen. But not until the mid-19th Century were there any cafés that provided the opportunity to spend evenings out in a family setting. The first—or at least the first well-known—such institution was a coffee house named Krasnapolsky ("Kras" to Amsterdammers), situated behind Dam Square.

It often takes a foreigner or an outsider to discern the characteristics of a society and to give it exactly what it wants; and this establishment's founder, Adolf Wilhelm Krasnapolsky, was such a man. I have no hesitation in nominating him as the patron saint of all Amsterdam café-goers. A Polish immigrant, Krasnapolsky for a time worked as a linen cutter in a furnishings and drapery store. He saved up enough money to buy a defunct Polish coffee house in 1865. Putting his own stamp on the premises, he endowed it with a unique air of home-from-home, with rich plush furnishings and a menu that included *pannekoeken* (thin, large pancakes) made to a recipe known only to his sister-in-law. The place was an instant success, and Krasnapolsky personally ran it almost until his death 47 years later. During that time he introduced other novelties. His establishment was the first public place in Amsterdam with electric lighting and the first to install telephones. He also turned part of the premises into a palm garden where meals and drinks were served to the accompaniment of a small orchestra—an idea that has since been copied all over the world. A visit to Kras became a must for foreign visitors.

Another Pole, the novelist Joseph Conrad, immortalized the place in his book *The Mirror of the Sea.* Conrad, who called there while feeling depressed because his vessel was laid up overlong in Amsterdam harbour, wrote of "a gorgeous café in the centre of town. It was an immense place, lofty and gilded, upholstered in red, full of electric lights, and so thoroughly warmed that even the marble tables felt tepid to the touch. The waiter who brought me my cup of coffee had, by comparison of my utter isolation, the dear aspect of an intimate friend." With a true novelist's intuition, Conrad hit upon the essence of *gezelligheid.*

I should hasten to add that *gezelligheid* has not exactly been an all-conquering force in Amsterdam's nightlife. To see just how uneven the nocturnal ambience is, look at Amsterdam's squares, which would seem to be logical focal points for evening entertainments. Although Kras is still going strong, the Dam Square itself, in front of it, has had a certain cold gravity ever since the year 1808, when Louis Napoleon, who had been

Bending over a brimming, tulip-shaped glass, the proprietor of the Wijnand Fockink "tasting house" demonstrates the correct way to take the first sip of Dutch gin. Visitors to the establishment pay to sample some of the unique collection of Dutch liqueurs that crowd the shelves behind the bar.

made king of Holland by his brother, turned the Town Hall into a palace. It is now the Amsterdam residence for the reigning House of Orange, but none of the members of the royal family has used it for any length of time and its emptiness casts a pall on the area. Only during those years around 1970, when Dam Square was a gathering place for the hippies of the world, did this spot come to life in the thoughts and emotions of the town.

Another great city square, the Frederiksplein, once had cafés on all four corners and was actively *gezellig*; now it is quiet. In my childhood its central area was occupied by the Palace for National Industry, a huge iron-and-glass structure where concerts and meetings took place. The palace was destroyed by fire in 1929 and, after some decades of argument about what to put in its place (it is on such occasions that Amsterdammers show their individualism almost ad infinitum) the Netherlands Bank won out and built its main office there. Although such a building may be the result of an economic boom, it does not give visible cheer to the life of that part of town, especially after the last employee in the shops around the square has lowered the last blind at the end of a workday.

A third main square, Rembrandtsplein, has undergone much tearing down and rebuilding, partly as a result of wartime destruction. The only noteworthy establishment surviving from my own past (and the Rembrandtsplein had a brilliant past of cabarets and night spots in the 1920s and 1930s) is Schiller, a restaurant-cum-hotel opened in 1892 and nursed to greatness by Frits Schiller, who was the best cook among Amsterdam painters and the best painter among Amsterdam cooks. In the 1950s, Schiller's café terrace was eminently *gezellig*. Frits was supremely solicitous of his guests, and his grey head was constantly seen bobbing among the tables. He is dead now, but his paintings still hang on the walls, and if they inspire his successors to maintain the old spirit of the place, all will be well.

Adjacent to the Rembrandtsplein is another square dedicated to a locally famous son—a politician named Jan Rudolf Thorbecke, who in 1848 forced a liberal constitution upon a conservative parliament. Unfortunately for the memory of this Dutch Jefferson, Thorbeckeplein—which in my youth was a quarter with chic nightclubs and restaurants—has become a squalid centre of girlie bars.

I have saved the most renowned square for last. It is, "of course"—as anyone will say who has ever set foot in Amsterdam—Leidseplein (Leyden Square), in older times the terminus for stagecoaches travelling to and from Leyden. Leidseplein is to Amsterdam what Piccadilly Circus is to London, and what Times Square—minus the junkies and bums—is, or could be, to New York. It has everything: brown cafés (which I will deal with in a moment), the Municipal Theatre, one or two first-class restaurants, a good cinema, a discotheque, a couple of *broodjes-winkels* (those Dutch sandwich shops that serve dozens of types of cheeses and cold cuts in fresh buns) and, last but not least, the Americain—a hotel that also boasts a remarkable café.

Although I use the French-style name "Americain", the golden letters on the hotel's façade spell "American", and that is the establishment's official title in both the registers of the city and in the telephone directory. But just as no New Yorker will ever call The Avenue of the Americas anything but Sixth Avenue, no Amsterdammer will call the American anything but the "Americain", with the stress on the last syllable. In fact, the pronunciation of the name may be used as a shibboleth to distinguish Amsterdammers from all outsiders, be they from Leyden or from Seattle.

Since 1880, when it was built, the Americain has ranked as the heart of *gezelligheid* in the public life of Amsterdam. In spite of its old-fashioned décor—ornate arches, yellow glass lamps, wall paintings and stained glass windows—it is patronized by Amsterdammers of all ages and occupations, from students to city councillors, from housewives to fashion models. According to local lore, if you sit on the hotel's terrace for long enough, sooner or later you will meet everyone you know. In the evenings, the actors and actresses of the Municipal Theatre next door adjourn to the Americain to discuss the performance. If they are very young, they may even leave their make-up on; and some of the theatre-goers, having repaired to the same place for a late supper or a drink, may give them an encore of applause—once a firm tradition.

I would like to be able to say that the future of both the Leidseplein and the Americain are assured, at least in our lifetimes; but one has to be careful with such statements. A future proprietor may decide to replace the fine art-nouveau lampshades in the Americain with fluorescent strip lighting (easier to clean). More ominously, some very drastic schemes for demolition and reconstruction of the square and its surroundings have been bandied about. But perhaps cities and citizens are learning at last that it is easier to destroy an existing and viable neighbourhood or architectural entity than to create a better one.

I have earlier touched upon the subject of so-called brown cafés. These are an assortment of more-or-less dilapidated old taverns that were given a new lease on life when the postwar generation began to follow their elders' example and pour forth from their homes for evenings on the town. Because they are favoured by the young, it is fair to say that they are the scene of much of the artistic and intellectual life of the city.

The brown cafés probably derive their names from the colour of their wooden wainscoting and their generally dark interiors. They do their best to repel the uninitiated, and none that I know displays credit-card symbols, multilingual signs or neon enticements. By their nature and purpose, they are neighbourhood gathering places, somewhat in the style of the old-fashioned British pub. Unlike the ordinarily quiet pub, however, the clientele of a brown café often forms a throbbing throng, with everyone talking to everyone else. The establishments may remind some visitors of Paris café life of the 1920s, minus all the handshaking and the somewhat self-conscious bohemianism Paris then displayed. But instead of Pernod, the patrons mostly drink *pilsjes*, delicious glasses of draught beer of just the right temperature (to a Dutchman, all American beer is served too cold, all British beer too warm).

There is no sharp dividing line between these and other Amsterdam cafés, but the brown cafés are definitely a bit less family-like; many people stand rather than sit, and the noise level is often nearly deafening. Yet I don't feel that I am stretching my use of the word *gezellig* unduly when I maintain that the brown cafés are just as *gezellig* as the favourite sanctuaries of my generation. Some of them may have buckled under to the vogue of coloured posters and humorous or sexy graffiti, but mostly their décor is pleasantly nondescript. Typical furnishings consist of faded settees, wobbly chairs that have to be balanced by placing a beer coaster under one of the legs, a calendar somewhere along the walls, and little lightbulbs in coloured shades.

The name "brown café" is supposed to have been coined by the Amsterdam newspaper columnist Simon Carmiggelt, who made his reputation writing regularly about Amsterdammers and their habits, tending to describe his fellow citizens behind their *pilsjes* and *genevers* as detachedly as an ornithologist might describe the nesting rituals of sea gulls—but with obvious affection.

I knew Carmiggelt from my early journalist days. On my latest visit, having failed to run into him in any of his usual drinking spots, I went to

Bathed in an inviting rosy glow, two ladies-of-the-night sit in their own living-rooms awaiting visitors to Amsterdam's red-light district. Police check that prostitutes are older than 21 and Dutch; otherwise officials ignore long-established laws forbidding prostitution.

see him at his house. On that particular afternoon I happened to be suffering from generation lag: everyone in the cafés I visited had seemed so incredibly young, and old friends were difficult to find. Now I found myself poised to embark on a Proustian search for times lost and gone, and I mournfully announced, "Amsterdam is not the way it was."

"Well," he answered, "I'm not the way I was either."

I realized I had allowed a touch of self-pity to stand in the way of honest social observation. Carmiggelt proceeded to assure me that his failure to show up at the usual haunts should not be construed as an ominous portent for Amsterdam café-life. He told me that here—as everywhere else—television keeps many people in their homes, but that it appears to affect the young blessedly little. His own grandson, he said, went out every night and came home full of ideas springing from hours of intense talk. Yes, crime was on the increase, but not to the point where it kept people off the streets (except for one or two notorious bad spots). In short, he insisted that the Amsterdam scene was as *gezellig* in all its implications as ever; only the players had changed. And if boys and girls start going out on the town at an earlier age than they did, say, 30 years ago, that was only the natural result of different social mores and different economics.

Still, certain fundamental changes in Amsterdam's public life have occurred since my day. One is the tremendous influx of foreign visitors. As a tourist attraction, Amsterdam is now more popular than any other European city except London, Paris and Rome. But the foreign visitors have altered Amsterdam not merely by their physical presence. For their benefit, or at least for the benefit of those who come from more circum-scribed societies, an entire new industry has arisen—an industry whose dubious products consist of sex paraphernalia, blue movies and live sex shows. The establishments purveying these items are concentrated in an area just east of the Zeedijk, or Sea Dike, where they occupy some of the loveliest 17th- and 18th-Century canal houses. So powerful are the few businessmen who have carved up this lucrative pie among themselves that the police do not enforce the statutes forbidding neon signs and advertising on the façades of such houses. "We've reached a compromise," an official from the town Public Works Bureau told me lamely. "They keep their signs below the second floor. And they do pay for the upkeep of the houses."

In the line of reportorial duty, I visited one of the live-sex palaces. I cannot confess to guilty excitement; the whole experience was sur-prisingly boring and rather disgusting. Most other visitors in the place appeared to feel the same way. And from neither the clientele nor from the personnel did I hear one word of Dutch, confirming what the Public Works official had told me: while located in the very heart of town, this whole business serves foreigners and has nothing to do with the daily life of Amsterdam. In any case, the sex palaces and kindred establishments are definitely not *gezellig*: every customer is alienated from all the other members of the audience by the fake intimacy of the spectacle, its wordlessness, and its embarrassing humiliation of the actors.

This is not a gratuitous observation, for—unlikely as it sounds—Amsterdam's own approach to commercial sex can, in fact, be seen as an example of *gezelligheid*. In the traditional red-light district of Amsterdam, homeyness and restlessness, comfort and adventure, all meet as in no other city in the world I know. Amsterdam has no legalized brothels, but what people want to do in their own homes is felt to be no one else's business. Amsterdam's ladies-of-the-night are private entrepreneurs, each sitting in the front window of her own little flat. There is little to distinguish the prostitutes from other Amsterdam ladies reading or knitting at their windows, except for a certain skimpiness of dress and for *schemerlampen* whose lightbulbs are a bit redder than is practical for reading purposes. They also favour lacy curtains that hang down in what might be described as stalactite patterns. In short, their attitude is decidedly middle-class. And while I certainly am not inclined to romanticize prostitution, I must admit that these girls—of whom I've known one or two—argue convincingly that their work is a job like any other, and financially more rewarding than employment as a waitress or switchboard operator.

By unwritten agreement with the law, they have not located themselves all over town; they've concentrated in an area called the Walletjes, or Little Walls—a name derived from the two high-banked canals delineating it: Oudezijds Voorburgwal and Oudezijds Achterburgwal. In the Middle Ages, these two canals formed the inner and outer walls defending the side of the fortified town. Today, at the very spot where the citizenry once repelled their besiegers (or, in bad years, were overwhelmed by them), Amsterdammers have a place where, in Albert Camus' words, "they can be there and not be there".

The Cameraderie of the Brown Cafés

Framed in the checks of window panes, chess players pursue an inter-generational match at the Het Hok café, a popular meeting place for devotees of the game.

Two seemingly contradictory facets of the Dutch character—a desire for privacy and a love of conviviality—are resolved in the homey surroundings of Amsterdam's brown cafés, so-called because of their plain wooden furnishings and nicotine-stained walls and ceilings. They are an integral part of the city's society where the Amsterdammer can relax with family and friends, watch live entertainment, play chess, cards, or billiards, or participate in other activities in which various cafés specialize. The favourite aids to conversation and concentration are pils beer and genever—the world's first juniper-flavoured gin, invented in Holland at the beginning of the 17th Century. The brown cafés have changed little over the years. They tend to be family concerns of long-standing—haunts of pure leisure that remain largely unaffected by social, cultural or political trends.

Taking her turn at the microphone, a Jordaner gives a rousing performance for fellow customers at the 100-year-old Two Swans café. Sunday-afternoon singalongs have become traditional among the café's working-class clientele, to whose fraternity an outsider is admitted with a fine mixture of cordiality tempered by reserve.

With heads bowed over their newspapers and journals, patrons enjoy the quiet, studious ambience of De Engelbewaarder. Because the establishment has always counted many authors and journalists among its habitués, it is commonly known as the Literary Café.

At the Café Huysman, a quartet of card-players settle down to a quiet midday game under the interested scrutiny of a fifth friend. Their table is covered with carpetry, a decorative touch favoured in many Amsterdam brown cafés—and in some private homes as well.

In the cheerful surroundings of his own café, the renowned Amsterdam folk singer Jan Bolle supplies accordion accompaniment for one of his risqué compositions, while a guest does the vocal honours. Like many of the brown cafés operated by colourful personages, this establishment has come to be known simply by the name of its proprietor.

5

A Tale of Two Neighbourhoods

Although visiting foreigners tend to think of the old centre of the metropolis as the essential Amsterdam, it represents only a small fraction of the city's area—and a unique fraction at that. Amsterdammers pay their foremost loyalty to their *buurt*, or neighbourhood. (The word *buurt* is short for *nabuurt*, which, like so many Dutch words, has the same root as the corresponding English term: neighbourhood.) While the centre is a naturally defined aesthetic and historical entity, it is not really a neighbourhood. Most of its houses now serve as business quarters rather than residences, and the comparatively few people who do live there are not "neighbours" in a sense that would be recognized by the occupants of any of Amsterdam's true *buurten*.

In the main, Amsterdam has been expanded over the centuries by the systematic development of defined areas. The many distinct units that make up the city's whole are easily discerned, since the streets of each newly developed *buurt* were often given related names. For example, there is a patch of painters' names in the Old South district, below Vondel Park. East Indies island names abound in the Indischebuurt, east of the centre. In the south-east, beyond the Oosterpark is an area where all the street names are South African.

No neighbourhood can be described as "typical", but I want to single out two of them—the Jordaan and the Jodenbuurt—for special attention. In a topographical sense, they are a pair, for they were built on opposite sides of the old centre in the 17th Century—the Jordaan to the west and the Jodenbuurt to the east. The former was once a vigorous working-class district, and the latter was where many of the Jewish Amsterdammers used to live. I say "once" and "used to" because the Jordaan, although it still exists, has changed in many respects, while the Jodenbuurt has vanished completely, wiped out during the Second World War—people and houses alike. Yet, altered or vanished though they are, the stories of both are vital to an understanding of present-day Amsterdam. The city would not be the same place if they had not existed and contributed to its life, lore and values for upwards of three centuries. The Jodenbuurt deserves close consideration for an additional reason: its destruction was a major trauma in Amsterdam's history, and it must figure in any book that pretends to give an account of the city's character.

The Jordaan proper is bordered by the Brouwersgracht to the north, by the Lijnbaansgracht to the west, by the Prinsengracht to the east, and by the Passeerdersgracht to the south. The northern half of the district, beyond

Lingering in the late afternoon sun, a woman gazes out from the steps of her home on the Herengracht. A majority of the 17th-Century houses in the area have been converted into offices, but old-fashioned street lamps and an abundance of flowers preserve an atmosphere of neighbourly charm lacking in other city centres.

the Elandsgracht, is the most authentic and unchanged, and much of the Jordaan feeling spills over from it to the east of the Prinsengracht.

As in other neighbourhoods, street nomenclature underlines unity. Many of the thoroughfares and byways have flower names, and—as if there weren't enough flowers in the world to name any number of streets —you will find, besides Anjeliersstraat (Carnation Street), such mouthfuls as Tweede Anjeliersdwarstraat (Second Carnation Sidestreet), and so on. Late in the 17th Century, numerous French Huguenot refugees settled here, and at school we were taught that Jordaan is a corruption of the French word *jardin* (garden), inspired by all those flower names. But serious scholars have been picking holes in that story; they tell us that the stretch of the Prinsengracht between the Brouwersgracht and the Passeer-dersgracht used to be called the Jordaan, after the holy Jordan river, and that the inhabitants along that length of canal called their area the Jordaan for that reason. Perhaps the Huguenots misunderstood the Dutch name, making both explanations true.

Throughout the 18th and 19th Centuries, the Jordaan became in-creasingly overcrowded, teeming with poverty-stricken workers, many of whom were—like the Huguenots—immigrants taking refuge in liberal Amsterdam from political or religious oppression elsewhere. Most of the workers were engaged in grimy or unskilled trades such as tanning, tinker-ing, peddling. (Hartenstraat, the Jordaan street where I lived after the war, originally took its name—Deer Street—from the malodorous deer-hide tanneries that functioned there in the 17th Century.) This society always had room for a few artists, printers, sculptors and intellectuals who were attracted by the cheap living and informal ways to be found there. The 17th-Century map-maker, Johan Blaeu, produced his exquisite atlases (sometimes worth $40,000 or more to modern collectors) in a Jordaan house on the Bloemgracht where he and his father Willem kept a shop; Govert Flinck, one of Rembrandt's best-known pupils, lived near by; and Rembrandt himself moved to the Jordaan in 1660. More recently, the painter George Hendrik Breitner, who died in 1923 after living in Amster-dam for nearly 30 years, lived along the Lauriergracht, a broad street in the southern half of the district.

Well on into the 20th Century, typical conditions in the Jordaan re-mained appalling, with whole families living in one-room squalor. Yet the miserable housing and other shared adversities bred a compensatory humour and conviviality that became the hallmark of the neighbourhood. Isolation, too, played a large role in giving Jordaan life a special flavour. Not until 1908 did the Jordaan have a proper connection with the inner city, by motor bus. But the exhaust fumes of the buses blackened the washing that hung (as it still does) along the house-fronts, and there was so much protest that the route was dropped after a few months. The Jor-daners had to wait for the construction of an electric tramway in 1924 to

Two housewives in the heart of the old town avail themselves of the most convenient venue for the exchange of neighbourly gossip—the windows of their flats.

get acceptable public transport "into town". As a result of its history of separateness—either enforced or voluntary—the Jordaan had long since become almost a distinct nation within the city. Its inhabitants displayed numerous characteristics and customs of their own: special dress, slang, songs and professions. While some of these idiosyncracies remain intact today, others have been blurred by the mass trends of the 20th Century.

Among the local habits that have been progressively disappearing is the distinctive Jordaan style of dress, which was still common in the 1920s. Within the quarter, the women wore heavy baize skirts and white or black jackets, with leather slippers. On weekdays the men dressed in sweaters and corduroy trousers, and on Sundays they donned dark-blue suits with black watch-chains, light-hued footwear (usually yellow), a dicky with a paper collar, and a black linen skipper's cap. You have to search for old folk these days to find this get-up, but it is still around. All the children used to wear wooden shoes, which were given out free to the poorest children at the Jordaan public schools.

Many of the occupations that were traditional in the Jordaan have, of necessity, disappeared with the changing times. Not even the Jordaan can now offer a living to street-callers selling oat husks (to fill pillows) or carbolic stone (a primitive disinfectant said to work wonders in ridding a home of fleas and cockroaches). Nor can a livelihood nowadays be won by cleaning out privies, sorting coffee beans, shelling shrimps, repairing pots and pans, peddling hatboxes or goldfish, or hiring out as a "knocker-up"—a job that entailed waking people at fixed hours by knocking on their windows with a long pole. And while Amsterdammers still love strawberries and smoked sprat, just as they always have, the days are long gone (and a good thing too) when you could hear the early-morning call of the Jordaners pushing a cart and singing out, "Fresh strawberries, 20 cents a basket," or "Sprats, ten cents a bunch" (a Dutch cent was the equivalent of about four U.S. cents).

One Jordaan-based activity that has retained a measure of its old vigour is the playing of barrel-organs in the street, in return for the contributions of passers-by. For a century, most of Amsterdam's barrel-organs have been rented from a shop with a Jordaan address: 19 Westerstraat (formerly Anjeliersgracht). Successive generations of proprietors there have kept the instruments in good repair and created punched scrolls of the latest tunes for them to play. Eight of the instruments are still in operation.

These barrel-organs—huge machines encrusted with drums, bells, statues and colour pictures of famous battles—used to be as characteristic of Amsterdam as its gables, although there were never more than 30 or so of them. In the old days it took three men to run a barrel-organ; one turned the handle that operated the machinery and two collected money on each side of the street. All three were needed to move the instrument from place to place. Some of these men had musicians' permits from the Town Hall, but others operated illegally. The latter were called *lef* runners—*lef* being slang for courage.

Turning the organ handle was not just a mechanical job, since each piece of music demanded its own rhythm and speed. My mother taught me: "Never pass a good barrel-organ by," and she would willingly stop in the rain to dig out a coin for a deserving team. Unfortunately, few street musicians want to turn those handles any more, so most organs are now powered by little gasoline engines. I am in favour of eliminating grinding jobs, but there is something idiotic about a barrel-organ—not a social necessity, after all—sitting in the street by itself with a combustion engine inexorably turning its handle at an unchanging speed. Feeling that my mother would agree, I now do tend to pass them by. Others evidently share my view of the value of a sympathetically operated barrel-organ: I recently saw an organ labelled with the proud claim, "Turned by hand."

One should never forget, of course, that organ grinding, along with street peddling, sprang from desperate penury. For that reason, the diminution or total disappearance of such professions should not be mourned. Yet, if the hardships that moulded the Jordaan have eased, the neighbourhood solidarity that grew up in reaction to those hardships has proved surprisingly durable. Jordaners cherish their neighbourhood almost possessively; in fact, all Amsterdammers regard the district with an affection amounting to sentimentality.

What is it about the society of the Jordaan that stirs such feelings? Many attempts have been made to describe the norms of this unique district, and inevitably a complex picture emerges. Jordaan society has been called a matriarchate: old women, generally addressed by everyone as "Grandma", have a special independence and dignity here. They go out alone to the cafés at night—something you won't see elsewhere in town. Family feeling is strong, and children are treated with much love and care; I was told by police experts that they rarely encounter cases of child neglect in the Jordaan. The police also told me that when there is a fight in the district, no one will phone the cops, as they would east of the Prinsengracht; the issue is settled by the people among themselves.

On the whole, Jordaners are easy-going and not mistrustful of outsiders; but they have a very sharp nose for pretentiousness, and their humour may turn a bit too earthy for the taste of the rest of the town. When I lived in the Jordaan, I once walked a friend home along the Rozengracht. This man had a beard, most unusual at the time, and during our walk someone dumped a pail of potato peelings out of a window on to his head with the cry, "Here, goat!" to the merriment of the local citizenry.

Another distinguishing trait of Jordaners is their mode of speech, known simply as Jordaans. It is characterized by verbal inventiveness, and a lively, punning volubility. Most Amsterdammers appreciate this playful slang, but the style does not necessarily travel well. I heard a sad story of a jovial Jordaan butcher who moved to Utrecht: his stream of jokes, puns and repartee all fell flat with the unresponsive Utrecht housewives, and he became something of a melancholic after a while.

The Dutch language boasts a wealth of proverbs and sayings, and Jordaners are especially fond of them. Because of their colloquial and non-literary character, these sayings often become very flat in translation; but in the Jordaans accent, they carry the ring of blunt truth—especially for children. To quote just two examples from the realm of pedagogy: "children who say 'I want' get a spanking"; and "choosy pigs don't get fat."

If the Jordaners' predilection for proverbs is very Dutch, there is something almost Latin about their love of music and singing. The delight they take in street dancing is particularly unusual in Holland, especially in the northern provinces: you will find dancing in the cafés of the Jordaan, but none in the city's other districts (except in discotheques). Jordaan songs exploit pathos—and bathos too. They treat of young love spurned or abused, jealousy, abandoned mothers, children's graves. Jordaan singers do these plaints enthusiastic justice.

Perhaps the same sentimental strain is at the bottom of a rather surprising—if sometimes misunderstood—attribute of the Jordaan. It is part of the romantic myth built around the district that its people are ardently in favour of the monarchy. They did, in fact, have special affection for old Queen Wilhelmina, who was a kind of grandmother figure, possessing an obvious devotion to "the people", and even a sense of identification with them. Maybe some of that affection was generated by the shared tribulations of the Second World War. But the Jordaners are basically hard-headed and the Jordaan has habitually voted solidly socialist and included a significant number of communists.

The anti-government feeling of the district, always ready to ignite, resulted in riots in the 19th Century and again during the Great Depression of the 1930s. I myself remember the rebellion of 1934—small potatoes in international terms but a big thing in pre-war Amsterdam. Sparked off by a government decision to lower the dole in the midst of the rigours of the Depression, it began with a march of unemployed men that turned into a riot. When the police arrived, the Jordaners showered them with paving bricks plucked from the streets. Barricades went up and the army was called in to restore peace. For several days the beleaguered Jordaners kept police and troops at bay; by the time order was finally restored, six people had been killed and 30 injured. The Jordaan gained nothing by the outbreak—except an ironic modernization: to remove the district's handy weaponry, city authorities replaced the old-fashioned brick paving with asphalt.

The Jordaan spirit has since shown itself in other causes. It flared up in the historic strike of February, 1941, against the Germans, which I shall

In a Jordaan street that once rang to the cries of fish vendors and pedlars of pots and pans, shoppers stroll past boutiques and snack bars. The passing of the colourful old merchants is lamented by some Jordaners, but the new businesses have revived the fortunes of Amsterdam's poorest neighbourhood.

shortly get to; and in the early 1970s it came into play in opposition to a civic scheme that threatened to alter the district beyond recognition.

In 1969, the municipality drafted a detailed redevelopment plan for the district and presented it to the public for approval. Town planners have always been an active breed in Amsterdam, and it was only too tempting for them to presume that all those little old houses in the Jordaan should be razed and the people made happy in high-rise buildings amid a sea of traffic. The plan would have caused massive dislocations, since most residents would have been unable to afford the relatively high rents for the new housing, even though it was to be subsidized. The proposal also would have replaced the local mixture of shops, businesses and houses with an artificially neat segregation of residential and commercial zones.

Vociferous complaints were made, both by Jordaners and citizens elsewhere in the city. The first plan was withdrawn and by 1973 a new version finally agreed upon. There was to be less demolition and more gradual replacement of buildings without the wholesale displacement of their occupants; funds were to be made available for restoration of decrepit buildings; large rent subsidies were to be forthcoming to help old Jordaners stay in their restored houses; and housing and shops would remain intermixed so that the neighbourhood would retain its character as a self-contained world where everything was within walking distance.

On my latest visit to the area, I gained the impression that these good intentions were indeed being realized. Before venturing to the district, I had heard rueful comments about the chic art galleries, expensive boutiques and fancy speciality shops that were invading the Jordaan, once so solidly working-class. Sure enough, they were quite visible. Yet to me their proprietors are worthy-enough successors to the resourceful crafts-men and street-callers of the previous centuries. It is sweet and nostalgic to read about the old Jordaan, where you could buy a pair of re-soled, second-hand shoes for 60 Dutch cents (20 U.S. cents), and when a tailor would turn your suit for a guilder. But one can hardly complain about commercial trends that bring prosperity without unravelling the funda-mental look and feel of a neighbourhood. The people selling paintings, tight jeans and kegs of Spanish sherry are the keys to a remarkable economic somersault. Without them, the Jordaan would surely have died in the long run, for no community can afford to become a museum.

The Jodenbuurt district has no such dilemma about the form its survival is to take, since it no longer exists at all. But until its extinction during the Second World War, the Jodenbuurt, like the Jordaan, greatly contributed to the city's language, humour, culture and character. In this neighbour-hood—which lay to the east of the old centre, between the Oudeschans Canal and the Zoo—Jewish immigrants of all periods traditionally settled. The poorest of the residents used to live around Waterlooplein; farther east, in a section called the Plantage (Plantation), the houses were larger, the streets wider, and the people more well-to-do. As in the Jordaan, a strong sense of community existed in the Jodenbuurt, but it was based on religion and custom rather than working-class solidarity.

The name Jodenbuurt means simply "Jews' quarter". But this bald labelling of the district does not mean that it was a ghetto or a "separate world". Religious prejudice has always been quite foreign to the mentality of Amsterdam, and so there has never been a need to cloak it under circumlocutions or for Amsterdam's Jews either to seek or to avoid identification. The question simply does not arise. For instance, one of the great Amsterdammers of the 19th Century was a man named Samuel Sarphati; in school we learned that he was a promoter of public housing, an organizer of municipal services such as garbage collecting, and the builder of a bread factory that provided better and cheaper bread for the city (he also built the Amstel Hotel). We were taught about Sarphati because he was a great philanthropist; I never knew he was Jewish—until the German army arrived in Amsterdam and the German authorities changed the name Sarphati Street into Muiderschans, a local name chosen to match the adjacent Muidergracht and Muiderpoort.

The editor of an Amsterdam weekly, a friend of mine, once angrily fought against a (well-meant) initiative to ban the Amsterdam word *voddenjood*, which means "rag-and-bones Jew", and change it to *voddenman*, or "rag-and-bones man". In Amsterdam, he wrote, a man collecting rags and bones was traditionally a Jew, and not interested in hiding that fact either. The editor was a Jew himself.

I am just touching on what is admittedly a complex phenomenon. It should not be thought that I want to paint the Amsterdammers as too good to be true, and I do not want to imply that anti-Semitism was entirely unknown here. When the 1930s brought an influx of new Jewish refugees from Germany, there was a lot of unpleasant comment. However, the hostility of Amsterdammers was really aimed at the German, not the Jewish, character of the newcomers. They had what we called a *bei-uns* ("in our country") complex; the real nature of Nazism had not yet been quite recognized by its first victims, and the immigrants spoke about how, *bei-uns*, things were done more efficiently than in Holland.

But these were petty irritations, wiped away forever by a massacre that utterly appalled all Amsterdammers. After the German invasion in 1940 and the imposition of Nazi racial policies, the first reaction of the Gentile populace was: "They can't do that to *our* Jews." I've heard those very words spoken by many Amsterdammers. And many Dutch Jews failed to hide or escape because they, too, felt that the Germans would not dare differentiate between them and their fellow Amsterdammers. The ensuing horrors were made all the more tragic by the fact that they took place in a city that for centuries had been known for the protective welcome it extended to people of different faiths.

The first Jews in Amsterdam were Sephardic merchants who arrived in the 16th Century. They came mainly from Portugal, where the Inquisitors had sought to wrest away their control of the thriving trade between the Iberian peninsula and northern Europe. Some of them had first transferred their activities to Antwerp, but when that city fell to Spain in 1585, they—along with a large number of Protestant merchants— moved to Amsterdam to escape Catholic persecution. Later they were joined by a host of new arrivals direct from Portugal and Spain.

Some of these Iberians were families of substance, and we find their names among the shareholders in the East and West India Companies. At first they did not have the same rights as other inhabitants of the city; for instance, certain trades and professions were closed to them, and they were forbidden to inter-marry with Christians or to employ Christian servants. Still, they enjoyed exceptional freedom in comparison with Jews in other European cities, for Amsterdam was particularly conscientious in upholding the pledge of religious freedom made by the Protestant provinces of the nascent Dutch Republic in 1579, as they struggled towards independence from the imperialism of Catholic Spain. For example, around the year 1600, when Christian property-owners pointedly requested that the Municipal Council pass a by-law "determining the places within this city where the Jews will be allowed to live", the council replied that Jews could live wherever they wanted.

"Freedom of religion", as spelled out in Article XIII of the treaty that effectively founded the Dutch Republic, meant that no one would be bothered or persecuted because of his religious beliefs. It did not mean freedom to conduct religious services openly; that was said to be a civil matter of maintaining public order. Soon after the Protestant republic was set up, Catholics started holding their services again, but they took the precaution of doing so in *schuilkerken*, hidden sanctuaries. The Jews, for their part, had an alarming moment in the year 1603, when the city authorities interrupted a Yom Kippur prayer meeting in Jonker Street and arrested Uri Halevi, the first Amsterdam rabbi. However, it turned out that the action was prompted by a report that Spaniards—the enemy, since the Republic was still at war with Spain—were conspiring there: because most of these Jews had Spanish names and spoke Spanish or Portuguese, the authorities mistakenly believed that their target was a Spanish conclave. Rabbi Halevi was released when it became clear that he was not leading any "Papist plot". After 1630, the Jewish community was left to hold services in peace. The Portuguese Synagogue, built on Jonas Daniël Meijerplein between 1671 and 1675, far from being hidden, was and is one of the most striking buildings in Amsterdam.

It was not merely humanitarian liberalism that made Amsterdam treat the Jews reasonably and accept them into the city. They were astute merchants who played an important role in the success of the Indies trading enterprises—so much so that the authorities went to considerable lengths to encourage them to stay in the city. The government upheld decisions of the Jewish elders, so long as they were not in conflict with Dutch laws. Jews were permitted to carry on those trades—such as that of kosher butcher—necessary to a full religious life. And their marriages were legalized and respected.

In the first half of the 17th Century, the number of Jews in Amsterdam was swelled by a steady stream of refugees from Germany. They were escaping from the persecutions that accompanied the political and religious struggles of the Thirty Years War, which disrupted most of Europe between 1618 and 1648. Groups of Polish and Lithuanian Jews, belonging, like the Germans, to the Ashkenazic sect, followed in the 1650s. These Ashkenazic Jews were mostly very poor, often destitute, lacking the education and contacts of the Sephardim.

The Ashkenazim, many of whom became street vendors and pedlars, were the target of much hostility from Dutch Christians; but municipal policy in Amsterdam remained liberal for the period. Although from 1668 on the Jews were not allowed to carry on crafts and trades controlled by guilds, these restrictions were not strictly enforced. Brokers', booksellers' and surgeons' guilds admitted a few, and St. Peter's Guild of Fishmongers never discriminated against them. In 1748 a decline in the city's important diamond industry, which had no guild and was dominated by the Jews,

RIJKSMUSEUM, AMSTERDAM

"The Jewish Bride," one of Rembrandt's most beautiful works, was probably commissioned in 1665, when the great artist lived in the Jodenbuurt—the Jewish quarter. The Sephardic couple are depicted as figures from the Old Testament—perhaps Isaac and Rebecca.

put many Christian diamond workers out of work. They demanded the institution of a guild in the industry so that Jews could be excluded or restricted, but the government refused, on the grounds that it was the Jews who had created the diamond trade.

Amsterdam's treatment of Jews differed from that of some other parts of the Dutch Republic. When I visited the new Jewish Museum in the Nieuwmarkt Weigh House, I came upon a crudely printed proclamation, issued during the 18th Century in Overijssel, in the east of Holland, threatening death to "Jews who wear arms" and to farmers giving shelter to "Jewish gangs". There is no evidence that the threat was ever carried out. Apparently, the poster reflected a temporary panic such as can sometimes occur among ignorant rural populations: the "Jewish gangs" were probably pedlars going from farm to farm with ribbons and combs and needles. Yet the poster is a useful reminder that, even in Holland, the phantoms from the dark side of the human heart sometimes lie in wait.

The presence of the Jews in Amsterdam brought the city other distinctions besides financial ones. Rabbi Menasseh Ben Israel, the successor to Uri Halevi, founded a Hebrew printing press in Amsterdam and in 1627 produced the very first printed Hebrew book of prayer. The importance of this publishing event went far beyond the local Jewish community: Hebrew was the language of the Bible and of powerful philosophical works; soon, Hebrew books printed in Amsterdam spread all over Europe.

Amsterdam also began publishing books—in French, Latin and other languages—that had been banned elsewhere. These were smuggled into other countries, often bearing on their title-pages the words "Published in Eleutheropolis"—that is, "in Freedom City".

For many years Rembrandt lived across the street from the home of Rabbi Menasseh. The two men were friends, and Rembrandt drew four illustrations for Menasseh's philosophical treatise *La Piedra Gloriosa* (The Glorious Stone), which was published in Portuguese and Hebrew in 1655. Thirty-five portraits of Jews further testify to Rembrandt's acquaintance with these cultivated people. And Rembrandt also left paintings of Biblical scenes that show how he gloried in the richness of the Sephardic ceremonies he knew: at the time, the rabbis still wore the purple or violet caftan of Sepharda (which means "Iberia" in Hebrew) and covered their heads with wide-brimmed Andalusian sombreros.

In the 18th Century, Amsterdam's Jewish community became the largest and most important in Europe. Large numbers of Ashkenazim continued to immigrate from eastern Europe; by 1795 there were just over 20,000 Ashkenazim in the city, versus 2,800 Sephardic Jews. In 1796, under the influence of revolutionary France, Holland erased all remaining legal discrimination against Jews. The Republic came to an end during the Napoleonic wars, to be replaced by a Kingdom of Holland, ruled by Napoleon's brother Louis. After the defeat of France in 1815, Holland remained a monarchy. Two years later, with the egalitarian intention of integrating the Jews into the population, William I, the first Dutch king, required that ordinary teaching in Jewish schools be done in Dutch. Religious teaching could be done in either Hebrew or Dutch, but Yiddish—a form of German spoken by most Ashkenazim—was forbidden, and consequently its use as an international *lingua franca* among Jews was greatly weakened. At the same time, however, the increasing use of Dutch by Jews helped to unite the Sephardic and Ashkenazic groups into a single society—albeit a complex and varied one.

In the Jewish Museum where I saw the Overijssel poster, the main exhibits are precious objects from synagogues. These gold and silver objects may give an impression of general prosperity that would be far from the truth. By the end of the 19th Century, when the city's Jewish population had reached 54,000, the Jodenbuurt could compete with the Jordaan for slum conditions. Picturesque it may have been, but that much-vaunted quality lay in the eye of the beholder: the hawkers of oranges, secondhand suits, or broken cups and saucers would have gladly sacrificed picturesqueness for decent clothes and a decent meal in their stomachs. Yet, as in the Jordaan, shared miseries helped foster a strong neighbourhood spirit, as well as a humour and a local slang that entered into the general language of Amsterdam. The Jews called Amsterdam *Makom* (meaning "the place" in Hebrew), and other Amsterdammers eventually

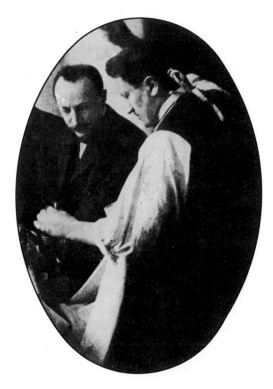

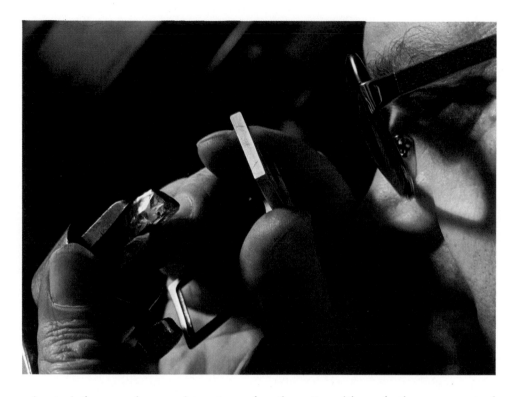

As a mark of Amsterdam's reputation for superb gem-cutting, the 3,024-carat Cullinan diamond —the largest ever found— was entrusted to the firm of Asscher in 1908 to be cut and polished (above). According to legend, the cutter was so nervous that he fainted with relief after making the first successful cleavage. At right, a modern-day craftsman in the Asscher workshop examines a rough diamond before it is to be cut.

adopted the word as a slang term for the city, although they corrupted the form of the word to *Mokum*.

By the 1930s, when I was a boy, the slums of the Waterlooplein area had vanished. There were decent schools and decent housing. Moreover, the Amsterdam municipal health service—free for anyone who needed it—was as good as science could make it. (I can speak from experience; my family, too, lacked the money to pay for private health care.) Yet, these benign changes had not diminished the old spirit of the quarter. Waterlooplein and the Jodenbreestraat (Jewish Broadstreet) still scintillated with life, and the Sunday morning markets in the Jodenbuurt brought people from the farthest corners of the city. Vendors there had pitches so artful that they could have sold a hairbrush to a bald man.

Apart from the street markets, the one other specifically Jewish sector of Amsterdam's economic life was the diamond industry. By this time, almost a third of the workers in the business were Gentiles, but almost all the important firms were owned and operated by Jews. These companies enjoyed a very high reputation throughout the world. The glittering showpiece of the industry was the Asscher factory, a place built in imitation of a medieval castle, its brick battlements complete with merlons and crenels. It was sited near the Amstel River in the Tolstraat, south of Sarphati Park and west of the area considered the Jodenbuurt proper. The workers lived around it on streets with such apt names as Emerald, Sapphire, or Topaz. These streets still exist and along them you can see housing that was remarkably good for industrial workers in the first half of this century. The men had themselves to thank for that. The General

Netherlands Union of Diamond Workers was one of the first of the strong Amsterdam trade unions, successfully fighting for the eight-hour day and a better deal all round.

I was told about the pre-war heyday of the diamond business by one of its survivors. There was much solidarity among the workers. "I'd call it brotherhood, if that is not too ponderous," he said. "We had all sorts of traditions, like going to the café on certain days, and every week we all took our wives to the Italian opera. Right from the beginning, we had been told by the foremen to read as much as we could. 'Education is power,' they said. We had our own library, and a fine one it was. My brother and I lived on Diamond Street. He didn't make it." So many of them didn't make it through the war that today only a third of the workers are Jews.

The essence of Jewish humour is perhaps a capacity for irony, a dismissal of life's disasters with a joke at one's own expense. If so, that tallied precisely with the mood of Amsterdam of the 1930s. Holland was poor, small and powerless against the vast political turbulence shaking the world. But because of its political neutrality, the country was also tranquil. Our disasters were minor, or at least they lay within the compass of normal human experience. But that would change with awful suddenness.

The Jodenbuurt that I have been describing was destroyed, quite literally, between 1941 and 1943. The German troops attacked Holland on the night of May 9, 1940, a Thursday. I recall it very clearly. I had been to a late movie, and as I bicycled home around midnight I could hear much distant rumbling of Dutch anti-aircraft guns. That was nothing unusual: for months Holland had demonstrated its neutrality by taking shots at any and all unidentified planes coming over. But the following morning my mother came into my room at about six o'clock and said, "We're at war." I lay in my bed and shivered and shook for a while, but then I calmed down, and such sheer terror never afflicted me again.

Out on the streets, people were already forming long queues at grocery stores and shoe shops. After all those centuries of peace, they knew almost instinctively what deprivations war could bring. Yet our powers of foresight soon revealed their limitations. We all thought there would be a static front line of trenches somewhere east of the Zuiderzee, and in school we discussed who'd be called up first. But this wasn't 1914; four days later the sky over Amsterdam was black with the smoke of the oil reservoirs burning; and a day afterwards the German columns marched through the city. The Dutch army had surrendered. No armistice was concluded—and there was no surrender by the Dutch government which, in exile, stayed at war with Germany.

In the autumn of 1940 the Germans promulgated the first of their anti-Jewish measures, dismissing all Jewish civil servants from their posts. In February, 1941, disturbances broke out between Jewish workers and

THE DE GROOT COLLECTION SANTPOORT, HOLLAND

Ignoring the rains of September, 1940, a defiant Amsterdammer clad only in hat, socks and shoes stalks across the Leidseplein in a one-man demonstration against the rationing of clothes imposed by Nazi authorities. Six months later, many citizens rose to protest against the first round-up and forced deportation of Amsterdam's Jews.

German and Dutch Nazis. On February 22, the Germans began retaliatory raids on Jonas Daniël Meijerplein. They rounded up at random 425 Jewish men under the age of 35; these men were destined for deportation to the death camps, although no one in Holland knew that yet.

In the new Amsterdam Historical Museum off Kalverstraat is a photograph that I have stared at often and for long periods of time. It was taken on February 22, 1941, almost certainly by an amateur, since it is not very sharp. It shows the crust of old snow in the square: the winter of 1940-41 was bitter cold, unending. German soldiers in helmets are standing around. The central figure in the picture is a Jew approaching the camera, who is evidently being herded somewhere. He wears a long blackish overcoat, a white shirt, and black bow tie. A waiter, a musician? We will never know, since none of the Jews arrested that day survived. A few steps behind this man walks a German, in the government-issued cap and belted overcoat we came to know so well. A pistol in his belt indicates that he is a sergeant or an adjutant. The man in the long black coat seems neither scared nor indifferent; there is an odd, hasty expression on his face. He is going through an experience utterly unknown in Holland and he looks as if he were taking stock of it. By contrast, the officer is smiling at the camera with the relaxed air of a holiday-maker having his snap-shot taken. He is no SS zealot, just an average member of the German army, thousands of whom came back to visit Holland after the war was over to show their wives where they had been stationed.

That photograph documents the destruction of Amsterdam Jewry in one glance. For me it has the elements of nightmare. I realize that now, so many years later, hatred serves no purpose, nor is it even acceptable. Still, I well understand an Amsterdam bookstore owner who still has a sign in his window stating, "We Don't Speak German."

Often, things can happen in one spot of the city and remain unnoticed everywhere else. But tram conductors and mailmen had seen the Meijerplein people being loaded, with open brutality, on to German army trucks. On February 24, city workers of all religions met and discussed a protest strike. Some individual communists—members of the secret but highly organized Communist Party of Amsterdam, which was particularly strong among the dock-workers—called a general strike. The following morning, no trams operated, no garbage trucks appeared, no mailmen stirred. Within hours, virtually every single factory, office and workshop in Amsterdam emptied. The city fell silent.

In the afternoon, the strike spread in a 10-to-15-mile circle around the city—to Haarlem, Zaandam, and the Hilversum area. The Germans declared a siege, dissolved the Municipal Council of Amsterdam, and sent troops all over town. Strikers were arrested and shot; within a few days the strike had been suppressed. But it had been the first and only time that the population of a city in occupied Europe went on strike—a capital offence against the Reich—in solidarity with their Jewish fellow-citizens.

After the strike, the deportation of Jewish Amsterdammers was taken up systematically and, tragic to say, under the orderly administration of some Jewish leaders who imagined that co-operation would ease things for most Jews. Of more than 80,000 Jewish Amsterdammers, almost 70,000 died in concentration camps. An estimated 12,000 Jews went into hiding, of whom about 7,000 were still free at the end of the war.

One of those who did not survive was Anne Frank, whose diary of a secret life in occupied Amsterdam—published in 1947—would stir the hearts of millions of people around the world. She and her family went to a now-famous concealed *achterhuis* (back part of a house) on the Prinsengracht on June 12, 1942, and were arrested there on August 4, 1944. Going into hiding—in Dutch *onderduiken* (literally, diving under water)—was practised not only by Jews, but also by men who had been called up for labour service in Germany, and by resistance workers. Vast numbers of people lived through the war in cupboards and attics, spending hours every night with little crystal radio sets that brought news via the BBC in London. Hiding was far from easy in a country as flat and open as Holland, and luck played a major part in survival. Those who hid the *onderduikers* also risked their own lives, of course. Some were eminently brave, while others demanded large sums of money from their guests. Wartime Amsterdam had its heroes, but inevitably it also had its cowards and its greedy or indifferent people.

I remember when the city learnt that a prominent Dutch Nazi officer had been shot dead early in 1943; there was general rejoicing at this

A bust of Anne Frank seems to peer wistfully out of a house on the Prinsengracht, where she and her family hid for almost two years, until their arrest by the Gestapo in 1944. Here, the Jewish girl wrote her unforgettable diary of life during the German Occupation. She did not live to see her 16th birthday, but the refuge—stripped to a poignant emptiness—has been preserved by the Dutch as a memorial.

news, for everyone was deeply ashamed of those Dutchmen who identi-fied themselves with the enemy. But the event was also shocking. It was the first political assassination to occur in Holland since 1672, when two leaders of an aristocratic faction had been murdered by a mob.

Ordinary Amsterdammers faced the challenge in whatever way seemed appropriate to them. Amsterdam boys have always been used to writing their own comments on posters. When the Germans posted bills saying, "Germany is Fighting for a New Europe", the boys wrote underneath, *"Doet U voor mijn geen moeite"*, which is Amsterdamese for "Don't bother for my sake". Had they been caught, they might have been shot.

It took me a full two years to escape the city; not until after Pearl Harbor were underground lines established to get students, ex-soldiers and other volunteers out so that they could form a new Dutch army contingent to fight with the Allies. My two years under German oppression were feather-light compared with the final phases of the Occupation, which lasted five long years, almost to the day. But while I was still there, it felt bad enough. Time seemed to stand still as German soldiers in a hundred kinds of uniform shunted around in buses, while their grey-clad female auxiliaries, whom we called "grey mice", bought up everything in the shops. All the cinemas featured a deadening fare of musicals and comedies. The resistance was only beginning then and the city seemed just to sit there, silent, dark, filthy, crumbling.

The life of the Jodenbuurt was extinguished by late 1943, when the last inhabitants were arrested. For the rest of Amsterdam, the nadir came in the winter of 1944-45, when 20,000 people died of famine, and tulip bulbs were considered a luxury—to eat, that is. The cold, too, took a terrible toll. In September, 1944, the Dutch railway workers had gone on strike and the river traffic had been halted in reprisal by the Germans; as a result, from that time until May, 1945, Amsterdam was without gas, electricity or coal. Perfectly respectable citizens entered the empty houses of the Joden-buurt to take away wood for burning; first chairs, doors, and doorposts, then floors and beams. The plundered houses collapsed, and for years after the war the derelict Jodenbuurt was a scar on Amsterdam's face.

I re-entered Amsterdam in May, 1945—a week after the liberation— riding on a truck of the Allied 21st Army Group. We had a load of whole-wheat bread in the back, picked up on the way north in Zeeland Province. At a stop, one of us impulsively took a loaf of bread and handed it to a boy standing in the street. Within a few seconds, a crowd had assembled, and an old man with an umbrella was grappling with the boy over posses-sion of the bread. That was hunger.

Piles of garbage covered the streets. The wooden blocks from between the tram tracks had vanished, burned for fuel. And the harbour facilities had been reduced to a pile of twisted steel. My mother was very thin but not starving; she still had some potatoes left from a bagful she had obtained from a farmer in April, in trade for winter clothes. Soon the café terraces were packed, although all you could order was a kind of sweet, purple concoction. Sipping that purple artificiality, Amsterdammers sat and held their breath, and slowly began to believe it was all over.

It took a long time for any recovery to come to the blighted area of the Jodenbuurt, but in 1953 the city took the first steps towards some kind of rehabilitation. A few blocks were rebuilt instead of being razed, and Amsterdammers—some of them Jews—began to move back into those haunted streets. But modern highways and the new transportation systems have since claimed great swathes of the district. And although Amsterdam's post-war population figure of a mere 13,000 Jews—survivors, returnees and new-born—has now risen to a registered population of about 15,000, there can be no doubt that the Jodenbuurt, with all its special qualities, is gone forever.

For me, the only adequate commemoration of that loss is to be found on the central avenue of the Plantage, where the Hollandse Schouwburg (The Dutch Theatre) formerly stood. This imposing building was the home of many long-running plays, particularly those of the turn-of-the-century Jewish dramatist Herman Heijermans, whose pithy dialogue and anti-romantic realism won him enthusiastic audiences year after year. Being in the centre of the Jodenbuurt, the theatre was chosen by the Nazis as the collection point for the arrested Jews. After the war it was unthinkable to use this hall of miseries once more for a theatre. In 1958, the city acquired it and tore the building down, preserving as a symbolic memorial only the façade and fragments of the four walls. Within the walls, a stark stone column rises under an open sky, and beside it grow an olive tree and an oleander from Israel. On a whitewashed section of the shell appear the words: "My soul melteth for heaviness; strengthen thou me according to thy word. Psalms 119:28."

This quiet, open quadrangle is the most eloquent war monument I have ever seen.

The Ordeal of the Occupation

PHOTOGRAPHS BY CAS OORTHUYS

Amsterdammers risk the firing squad to place flags and flowers on a rubbish dump where 29 patriots were shot after an attempt on the life of the local SS chief.

Through five years of German Occupation, Amsterdam fully earned the motto that was to be bestowed on the city by Queen Wilhelmina after the Second World War: "Heroic, Resolute, Merciful". Forced by mean circumstances to eat rats and to strip corpses of their clothes, the Amsterdammers not only endured, they hazarded their lives to protect fugitives from the Nazis. In 1943 a clandestine group of photographers began compiling a record of the Occupation so that the courage of the citizenry would not be forgotten. Cas Oorthuys, who took the pictures on these pages, was a founder-member of the group. He recorded Jews in hiding, documented the secret war of the resistance, and detailed the harrowing physical hardships. Oorthuys was caught and consigned to a concentration camp in 1944, but he survived to see Amsterdam liberated in May, 1945.

A Jewish woman cautiously emerges from the false floor of a closet—the only entrance to a cramped refuge.

Secret Lives of the Fugitives

Behind the visible surfaces of the city lived the *onderduikers*, or divers—the term for people who spent the Occupation in hiding. Usually Jews or fugitive resistance workers, they were supported by an elaborate organization that provided them with funds and ration books. By the summer of 1944, the attics, cellars and secret rooms of Amsterdam hid almost as many citizens as the Germans had been able to transport to the Third Reich for forced labour.

A Jewish couple pass the hours amid the clutter of their attic hideout in a Gentile home. Only the courage of their host stood between them and the Gestapo.

A resistance arms expert repairs a machine-gun magazine. On the table beside him is a captured Luger pistol.

The Weapons to Fight Back

Weapons made the difference between active and passive resistance, but for much of the Occupation nothing was harder to come by. Most arms were acquired by raids on police stations; not until after D-Day did Allied arms-drops solve the problem of supply. These images indicate how deeply photographer Oorthuys was trusted: had the pictures fallen into German hands, it would have meant execution for everyone who could be recognized.

Resistance workers cache a rifle and ammunition beneath a lavatory. Storing and distributing weapons was perhaps the most dangerous of all covert operations.

The latest resistance news rolls off a mimeograph machine. Women distributed the broadsheets.

A resistance forger with a heavy workload on his desk meticulously traces an official signature.

Getting Out the News

While most Amsterdammers learned of the day-to-day events of the war on hidden radios, underground newspapers also flourished. At first these were mainly mimeographed broadsheets, but printed editions became more common as the war went on. The same printing presses could be used to produce faked documents, although resistance workers preferred to steal genuine papers.

Using a clandestine radio built into a hollowed-out gazetteer, a member of the resistance tunes into a Free Dutch broadcast emanating from London.

In the deserted Jewish quarter, an Amsterdammer scavenges for wood in a derelict house.

Winter of Desolation

The winter of 1944-45 was Amsterdam's worst ordeal of the war. Deprived of electricity and coal, people gutted abandoned houses in the Jewish quarter for fuel. Cats and dogs vanished, soon to reappear in butchers' shops as "roof rabbit". In crippling weather, thousands of Amsterdammers died of hunger, cold and despair before the city could be liberated.

Risking confiscation of her precious bicycle for the sake of a few hours of heat, a woman hurries homeward with a door that has been taken from an abandoned house.

6

Art and Anarchy

The marriage in March, 1966, between Crown Princess Beatrix of the Netherlands and Claus von Amsberg, a German, was not popular in Amsterdam. Well before the event, city authorities were aware of the possibility of protests against this royal union with a man whose homeland had brought Amsterdam such grief in the relatively recent past. On the day of the wedding, the procession route through the city was lined by a precautionary force of policemen and of soldiers. But their presence proved an insufficient deterrent to trouble. As the bridal couple proceeded in state from the church, a smoke bomb was lobbed out of the crowd and exploded near their carriage. It was followed by another, then another. No one was hurt, but the incident sparked off a series of clashes between the police and young demonstrators that continued well into the night. And next day a new word appeared on the front pages of newspapers throughout the world: Provo—short for provocateur.

No so-called revolutionary group ever exploited publicity more successfully than Amsterdam's Provos; for the next three or four years they were rarely out of the local headlines, and their antics continued to attract international attention as well. From my home in New York, I followed their activities as, true to their name, they provoked with a vengeance. They provoked the city's police, politicians, civil servants and the Establishment in general. They provoked fury, bewilderment, frustration, admiration and above all—consistent with the character of the citizenry—amusement. They flouted convention by staging outrageous plays and "happenings", and they upset Amsterdam's more conservative artists by fighting a campaign to win state subsidies for painters. For a brief and heady period, during which they seemed on the verge of gaining real political power, the Provos and kindred groups stretched the city's traditional tolerance near to the breaking-point. To this day, their various legacies can be seen or sensed everywhere in Amsterdam.

The movement was started, appropriately enough, by an eccentric, self-styled magician, Robert Jasper Grootveld. During the summer of 1964, Grootveld took it upon himself to stage "happenings" every Saturday night around a statue known as "The Little Rascal", a bronze effigy of a jaunty lad sited on Spui Square. The ostensible purpose of these protests-with-jests was to campaign against smoking, and the statue was chosen as the weekly venue because it had been donated to the town by a local tobacco company. (Rumour had it that Mr. Grootveld was himself a heavy smoker, but apparently no one noticed the irony.) When students became interested in

Irreverently crowned by students with a tin pot, a bronze statue of an urchin—a favourite Amsterdam folk figure—grins across Spui Square. In the 1960s, it was chosen as a target for derision by anti-capitalist protesters because it had been donated to the city by a tobacco firm—and thus was said to symbolize the "exploitation" of society by large corporations.

the campaign, the Saturday night rituals took on a distinct political flavour.

In July, 1965, the first Provo manifesto appeared, written by Roel van Duyn, a philosophy student at Amsterdam University. It was a curiously despairing document. "We cannot convince the masses, we scarcely even want to," he wrote. "How anyone can place any trust in that bunch of apathetic, unenterprising, witless cockroaches, beetles and ladybirds is a mystery to me. If only we could be revolutionaries. But we are more likely to see the sun rise in the west than a revolution in the Netherlands. We know our actions are useless: we are quite ready to believe that neither [U.S. President Lyndon] Johnson nor [U.S.S.R. Prime Minister Alexei] Kosygin will listen to us, and for that very reason we are free to do what we like. We also know that a demonstration is of no use in the long run; that is why it is so important to get as much as possible immediately out of demonstrating."

Demonstrate they did. The first protests, prompted by the announcement of Princess Beatrix's engagement, were anti-monarchist; but by the time the smoke bombs were thrown during her wedding, the Provos had also embraced the ideals of the international New Left and were determinedly opposed to the war in Vietnam, pollution, consumer-orientated capitalism, and the multi-party political system. This was standard revolutionary fare. But the Provos were markedly different from similar radical groups elsewhere; their protests were cheerful affairs. The demonstrators painted their faces like clowns and attacked the police with sly good humour rather than physical force. On one occasion, when the increasingly frustrated Amsterdam police tried to break up a happening with their rubber truncheons, the Provos retaliated with sticks of rhubarb.

It was such tongue-in-cheek tactics that generated the world-wide interest; and the intense Press coverage in turn gave the impression that the Provos were more numerous and better organized than was actually the case. In fact, there were never more than 25 or 30 persons who devoted their full time to arranging jovial harassments, but on the streets their numbers were swelled by sympathizers and sometimes simply by passers-by who became involved in the theatrical goings-on.

But not all their provocations—named "ludic actions" (from the Latin word *ludere*, to play)—ended without retaliation. Their infuriating habit of thumbing their noses at authority caused the frustrated police to over-react and wade into the Provo ranks with disproportionate violence, thus damaging the public image of authority and improving that of the Provos. The movement was provided with its first alleged martyr when a student was jailed in 1966 for merely handing to a policeman a Provo pamphlet protesting against the harshness of the local peacekeeping measures. Before long, a girl was accorded similar status when she was inexplicably arrested for the equally inexplicable action of handing out handfuls of raisins to passers-by in the street.

Smoke bombs, thrown by Provo agitators, greet the newly married Princess Beatrix of the Netherlands and Claus von Amsberg as they leave the Westerkerk on March 10, 1966. Objectors to the royal alliance with a German also addressed the bridegroom with cries of "Give me back my bike"—a sarcastic allusion to German confiscation of bicycles during the Occupation more than two decades earlier.

ASSOCIATED PRESS

By June, 1966, however, events assumed a new and ugly complexion. A man collapsed and died of a heart attack while participating in a demonstration by construction workers. (The workers were protesting against a reduction in pay for work done during holidays.) Next day, the demonstrators—supported by a large contingent of Provos—stormed the offices of an Amsterdam newspaper that had attributed the man's death to the workers themselves. The police moved in and the resulting street clashes around Dam Square continued for three days and nights.

Against this background of growing violence, the Provos were modifying their original nihilist philosophy and attacking the Establishment on its own ground. Two weeks before the construction workers' demonstration, Provo candidates stood for election to the Municipal Council—the body that rules the city, employs 30,000 civil servants, and controls an annual budget of more than a billion dollars. The Provos polled more than 13,000 votes, enough to seat their first representative, Bernhard de Vries.

If Provo behaviour on the streets was bizarre, the proposals enunciated in the council by De Vries were serious enough. He and other members of the movement drew up a detailed programme of so-called "white plans" to deal with traffic, housing and pollution problems: white-painted bicycles, donated by Provo volunteers, would be distributed throughout the city to be used and then left by whosoever needed them; white, electrically-powered cars would be made available to subscribers on a similar "use-it-and-leave-it" basis; white-painted chimneys would symbolize an end to industrial pollution; and housing earmarked for destruction would be painted white and made available to squatters. Sadly perhaps, most of the schemes came to naught. The white bicycle plan was the first casualty. The few bicycles donated by the would-be reformers disappeared within a few days of being put on the streets.

The white car plan did come to fruition—and with municipal support. But it was eight years before the first battery-driven vehicle appeared in the city. Its designer, a Provo engineer called Luud Schimmelpenninck, had dreamed of 1,500 two-seater Witkars—literally "white cars"— operating from 15 stations throughout the city. His idea was that subscribers to the scheme would pay a membership fee entitling them to a car key. When they wanted to use a Witkar, they could go to the nearest pick-up point, insert the key into a lock on the post to which the car was connected, and feed their destination into a computer that was electronically linked to all the other Witkar stations. The computer would then check to ensure that the car's batteries were charged, that there was parking space free at the destination and that the client was credit worthy. If all these probes were positive, the computer would automatically release the car and unlock its door so that the subscriber could drive away.

The moment the car was released, its meter would start, clocking at a rate of about three-and-a-half Dutch cents a mile. Charging by time rather than by distance, Schimmelpenninck calculated, would encourage members to drive at the vehicle's top speed of 20 m.p.h., thus allowing as many subscribers as possible to use the scheme. The meter would stop when the key was inserted in the lock at the other end of the journey, and the charge would automatically be entered on the member's account.

In fact, when the first 15 Witkars were put into service in 1974, none was computerized: each depot had to be manned by an attendant who collected the hire charge from the would-be driver. Nor were Schimmelpenninck's hopes for 1,500 vehicles even remotely realized; two years later a total of only 35 Witkars were operating. In spite of the Amsterdammers' initial enthusiasm for the scheme, motorists spoke disparagingly of these "pickle jars on wheels" and bemoaned their tendency to run out of power halfway through a journey. Conventional automobiles—for all their noisiness and polluting traits—remained in the ascendant.

By that time, the Provos themselves had vanished from the public scene. As far back as 1967, some Provos believed that their anarchist philosophy

On June 14, 1966, a cordon of riot police faces angry construction workers and their Provo supporters near Dam Square. The confrontation, which erupted into full-blown riots, occurred because the police were believed to be responsible for a man's death the day before, when the workers had demonstrated against a pay cut. In fact, the man died of a heart attack.

ASSOCIATED PRESS

had been betrayed simply because members had run for seats in the Municipal Council. In March of that year, Bernhard de Vries resigned his office; two months later, at a meeting in Vondel Park, Provo leaders announced that the movement was to be disbanded. The reason given for this voluntary demise was that things had become too organized, and organization was abhorrent to Provo ideals. With equally impeccable logic, many voices dissented on the grounds that it was not possible to disband a movement that had never been formally established. Whereupon, "the event turned into an indecisive happening", as a Provo publication put it.

In any event, a split developed between those members who renounced politics and politicians and those who continued to believe that their aims could be best achieved by declaring them from a platform of authority. It was not long before the latter splinter group became the *Kabouters*—Gnomes—a group that shared the Provo aim of making Amsterdam a cleaner, quieter city, but that was more serious in its political commitment. The Kabouters drew up plans for alternative ministries—one was to be a Ministry of Auto Elimination, another was to be the Ministry of Old Age Care. They also proposed the setting up of "urban farms", complete with geese and goats, that would put the townsfolk within easy touch of nature. They identified themselves by adopting a uniform: a little red pixie's hat.

In 1970, to the astonishment of Amsterdammers in general and the politicians in particular, no fewer than five of these Gnomes, led by the former Provo theorist Roel van Duyn, were elected to the 45-member Municipal Council. From the start Van Duyn set the tone for the group by arriving for meetings on a bicycle. At the official swearing-in ceremony, the five new Kabouter councillors shocked their colleagues by concluding the ceremony with a cry of "Suharto is a murderer"—an accusation aimed at the Indonesian head of state, who was alleged to have murdered communist rivals, and who was about to visit the Netherlands. In subsequent meetings, the more conventional councillors were astonished by Kabouter demands that all city buses should have gardens planted on their roofs.

Meanwhile, outside the council chambers, the Kabouters were showing the same instinctive flair for publicity as their Provo predecessors. They organized a mock burial of the official housing policy because it had failed to provide adequate homes for Amsterdammers (police stepped in just as a coffin containing a copy of the housing plan was being lowered into the ground). And they occupied empty houses, which had been condemned to make way for redevelopment, to make them available to squatters.

To many observers, the Kabouters seemed genuinely intent on achieving revolution in the traditional sense. In consequence, one newspaper correspondent predicted that a military coup in the Netherlands might be launched in order to forestall the forces of anarchy. In the event, the political reign of the Kabouters ended tamely.

One by one they resigned from the council, either in disgust with the

Battery-powered Witkars, available to the several thousand Amsterdammers who subscribe to a transport rental service initiated by the Provos, wait at one of the several pickup points around the city. The little vehicles—literally "white cars"—were designed to serve as an answer to pollution and parking problems created by petrol-driven automobiles.

entrenched views of their fellow-councillors, or simply out of boredom. Van Duyn's demise from power was different. In 1974, he left the Kabouters, joined the already existing Political Party of Radicals and was re-elected an alderman. In 1976 the council passed a motion of no confidence in him and he was forced to quit the Town Hall. It was an episode made memorable by a photograph taken at the time. It showed the bearded Van Duyn, in a sweater, sitting in front of two dapperly dressed councillors.

What, if anything, had the Provos and Kabouters achieved during their brief heyday? I put the question to a friend, an Amsterdam artist, one evening while we were sitting in a café on Utrechtsstraat, drinking Dutch gin and nibbling at cubes of cheese dipped in mustard.

He considered briefly before replying, and then said: "First, I think they introduced anarchist élan into the lives of ordinary citizens. This anarchism had no connotations of chaos or terror. It meant what it is supposed to mean according to the dictionary: self-imposed order.

"Of course," he continued, "it was naïve of those who thought the Provos were going to change society just like that. But the Provos did show Amsterdammers that a basic conflict of interest exists between the individual and the established interests of government and big business. And they demonstrated that one determined person using the right methods could tackle any organization."

I knew what he meant. As frolicsome anarchists, the Provos not only set people questioning hitherto accepted standards, they also set an example for people engaged in other, apparently unrelated struggles. One example was the women's movement. Amsterdam women had worked towards equality for decades, but they achieved startling results only after they began to adopt Provo methods. Like the Provos' attacks, theirs ranged from the serious to the crackpot. One group threw up picket lines, displaying such slogans as "Boss of my own belly", aimed at achieving the right to abortion on demand. Another faction marched through Amsterdam chanting, "We don't work for the fun of it", in order to galvanize city authorities into setting up free day nurseries for working mothers. Some women obstructed men's public toilets to establish the principle that there should be an equal number of public toilets for women.

Provo actions were also the magnet that drew thousands of back-packing young people to Amsterdam from all over the world. The Provos were exciting, unorthodox, absurd, amusing and irreverent—a heady and attractive mixture. For several years the youngsters had things their own way, sleeping out undisturbed on the steps of the war memorial in Dam Square and in shop doorways along the narrow streets near by.

But they, too, eventually fell foul of the Establishment. The issue that ended it all in the summer of 1970 was not even a serious one, such as the use of hard drugs (contrary to the demonology practised by some newspapers, there was very little of that): it was simply that the city fathers and shopkeepers tired of the fact that the entire city was being used as a camping ground. They had had enough of Amsterdam being labelled the "hippie capital of the world". As for the public in general, they felt the hippies were an alien, warm-weather presence. These youngsters looked different from the average citizen (although many citizens have since been imitating that look); and worse, they did not do any work.

The right to sleep out anywhere under God's heaven seems a basic one, but the shopkeepers around the Dam Square complained that they could not do business with people camping in their doorways; one merchant even installed water pipes so that he could "flush away" unwanted guests from his front step. At the end of August, the authorities banned sleeping out within the old town and the police were sent in to clear the square. In retrospect, it was a foolish decision; had it been delayed a month, the approach of winter—as well as the start of a new college year—would have done the job. Instead, running fights developed between the police and the youngsters, and continued all night. With the dawn, the result was still inconclusive—and so the city ordered tougher action. That night, detachments of the Dutch navy and marines took it upon themselves to occupy the square. Wielding leather belts, they forced the sleepers out of the plaza and the surrounding area. This time, the young people did not return.

To provide them with an alternative centralized campground, however, the authorities did make Vondel Park available for sleeping out—an arrangement that lasted for three years. Over that period, hundreds of thousands of young visitors spent nights in the park. Amsterdam tried hard to make the scheme work. About three-quarters of a million guilders (a quarter of a million dollars) was spent on toilet and washing facilities, baggage check-in arrangements, an information office, and an on-site medical clinic. The park became a huge open-air youth hostel, with messages pinned on trees, hundreds of brightly coloured bedrolls spread out on the grass, and washing draped over the fence that protected the statue of Joost van den Vondel, the 17th-Century poet and playwright for whom the park was named. Few of the campers were aware that Vondel had written lines that would be tailor-made for their philosophy: "Heaven is our roof; we do not work; we are as free as birds."

But by the nature of things, the Vondel Park experiment was a compromise that could not last. Amsterdammers living near the park complained of being kept awake all night by music; local hoteliers accused the hippies of pilfering the milk from their doorsteps; mothers with young children objected to picking their way through broken bottles—and worse. In January, 1975, Vondel Park was closed to campers, bringing to an end the era of Amsterdam as a hippie Mecca.

Dolls hanging from a wall form a bizarre mural near Waterlooplein. Its creator, a rag-picker, collected unwanted playthings for the purpose.

Up to a million young people still arrive each summer to "do their own thing", even if they are now forced to comply with the mechanics of city life. There are plenty of hostels and houseboats with inexpensive bunks, but it is not the same. A policeman told me that youngsters with sleeping bags still go into the park to try and spend the night, although they are moved on. "Some of them," he added, shaking his head, "have hundreds of guilders on them." He seemed to imply that only lack of money would compel a man to sleep under the stars rather than in a hotel.

While the Provo-inspired attempts to create an alternative life-style have fizzled out, they have had a lasting influence on Amsterdam's cultural life. From the beginning, the Provos drew support from the city's loosely knit community of writers, artists and political theorists. In 1970, for example, painters and sculptors staged their own "ludic action" by occupying, to the accompaniment of a flute, a wing of Amsterdam's Municipal Museum in order to lobby for state subsidies. Later, they organized a sit-in in the Rijksmuseum room that contains Rembrandt's famous "Night Watch"; but the museum director had the place cleared because, according to a teasing Provo pamphlet, he "feared the heated discussion would cause the temperature to rise so high that the painting might be damaged".

The painter Constant Nieuwenhys was an early Provo protagonist. In an essay written for *Provo* magazine, published from 1965-1967, he envisaged that automation would lead to increased leisure, and that the consequent release of social energy would be expanded in play—a form of creative activity that would make every man an artist in his own fashion. "The city of the future," he prophesied, "will no longer be a place to earn money, but to play in."

This idea nearly aligned with the Provo ideal that Amsterdammers should be left to pursue their individual interests, and with the logic that the people's representatives—the ones who controlled the purse-strings —should therefore provide the means to make that possible. In other words, the Provos felt it should be possible to have the best of both worlds: individual laissez-faire and social security. In the field of art, at least, they achieved their apparently contradictory ends by creating the climate that made it possible to extend the system of state patronage, known as B.K.R., which had been operating in a limited way since 1949.

Under B.K.R., which in Dutch stands for "Artist's Arrangement", most painters, sculptors, potters, weavers and graphic artists are now guaranteed that they will sell some of their work to the towns in which they live. Their art is bought with the help of a state subsidy, then exhibited in schools and public buildings. Prices are fixed in such a way that they give the artist enough to live on until the next sale—"enough" being defined as at least as much as a person would get under social security benefits, which are quite high in Holland. Thus, since the late 1960s, every halfway serious

TERRY SMITH

The neat façade of Rembrandt's home on Jodenbreestraat contrasts sharply with the ramshackle look of its neighbour, a junk store. Rembrandt lived in the house from 1639 to 1657, and it was here that he painted what is considered his best work, "Night Watch", a vibrant portrayal of civic guards.

artist has his or her livelihood assured, while some of the poorer bene-ficiaries even get a rent-free apartment or studio. All artists who apply to participate in B.K.R. are assessed by a jury, and few are turned aside. "If someone is rejected," I was told by a B.K.R. spokesman, "various appeals are possible. But if the jury errs, it is usually in the other direction. They do remember Van Gogh."

Vincent van Gogh sold only one painting in his lifetime, and lived for much of his life on the charity of his brother, Theo. Now, of course, his work is priceless. He paid only one visit to Amsterdam, and it was not a happy occasion. In 1881, at his home town of Etten, in southern Holland, he had met and fallen in love with a young widow named Kee Vos. She rejected his advances and returned to her parents in Amsterdam, where Van Gogh sought her out. Told by her parents that he could not see her, he thrust his hand into a candle and demanded to speak to her only for so long as he could endure the pain. Kee's horrified father blew out the candle and he and his wife took Van Gogh in charge. "Dear me," the artist wrote to Theo later, "those two old people went with me through the cold, foggy, muddy streets and they did indeed show me a very good, cheap inn." Belatedly, Van Gogh has found a permanent home of sorts in Amsterdam: in 1973 the city built a museum on Paulus Potterstraat to house works by him that are on permanent loan.

Curiously, the lessons of Van Gogh's poverty and despair have been lost on some contemporary artists, who frown on the principle of B.K.R. because they claim it "politicizes" their work. I consider this view to be nonsense. Only unrealistic romantics can believe that artists work best in a cold garret, on an empty stomach, and with the landlord hammering at the door. But I would agree that B.K.R. makes a difference in the end-product. Although there is no political pressure on participants, there is certainly an interaction between the social consciousness that created B.K.R. and the work of the men and women sustained by it: a significant number of the B.K.R. canvasses I have seen are devoted to such subjects as the horrors of war or visions of a nightmarish automated future.

Historically, the programme is not really a new idea. Some of the world's greatest art was done under a form of B.K.R.—except that it was called Church patronage or the patronage of the Medicis. Rembrandt, undoubtedly Amsterdam's most famous artist, relied on the patronage of the city's burghers—and their vain desire to be immortalized in oils—to meet the mortgage payments on his house in the old Jewish quarter, purchased in 1639. This home proved to be the scene of personal tragedy: three of his four children died in infancy and his wife died shortly after the birth of his son Titus. In 1657, unable to pay off even the interest on his mortgage, he was declared bankrupt and forced to move to rented accommodation in the working-class Jordaan neighbourhood.

Just as the Provos helped liberate art and artists in Amsterdam, so, too, did they haul the city's theatre and music into the modern ages. In my youth, Amsterdam was famous for its concerts, but there were few native composers whose work lasted. Furthermore, the theatre of the time could hardly be described as adventurous. The major event of the season at the Municipal Theatre—*the* stage as far as Amsterdam was concerned—was the New Year's Day performance of *Gysbrecht van Amstel*.

Gysbrecht is a rather fanciful historical drama about the rise of Amsterdam in the Middle Ages, and it was performed with a Greek chorus and much moaning and groaning on stage. It was written by Joost van den Vondel, who, schoolchildren learned, was a poor merchant dealing in silk stockings and that he was also the Dutch Shakespeare. The latter assertion is questionable, but *Gysbrecht* long ranked as Amsterdam's play laureate. It was traditionally followed by *Kloris and Roosje*, a comedy with rhymed jokes and New Year wishes to famous Amsterdammers.

Those were very "in" theatre evenings. When, wearing your Sunday suit, you were taken there for the first time by your parents on tramcars 1 or 2 (which still stop in front of the Municipal Theatre), it marked your début into the social life of the city—a cultural equivalent of a royal garden party in pre-war London. Most people think back to the event with a tender nostalgia, but I definitely recall being very bored. To me *Gysbrecht* seemed endless and, although I found *Kloris* rather amusing, neither play had any connection with real life—not even with the life of the age they were supposed to portray.

A student sketches in the courtyard of the Historical Museum, a former orphanage where some of the lockers (background) now advertise the treasures within.

The audiences of the late 1960s obviously felt the same way as I once did. Inspired by the Provos, a group of Amsterdam drama students—for no apparent reason calling themselves "Action Tomato"—vociferously interrupted performances at the Municipal Theatre to protest against the lack of social realism in its repertoire. Their actions eventually forced the theatre to defend publicly its choice and direction of plays. With that concession, the movement to bring drama to the masses grew apace. Today, it seems that the Arts in Amsterdam involve every man, woman and child over the age of 10. So many events are staged that a former bicycle garage close to the Municipal Theatre on Leidseplein has been converted into an information office to distribute programmes and leaflets detailing the numerous cultural activities that are available. During my latest visit, it took me an hour to read through the materials.

One of the leaflets prompted me to spend an evening at the Mickery Theatre on Rozengracht. The Mickery is a testing ground for productions from abroad: only foreign plays are performed there. The production I saw was wildly experimental, and at first I was irritated that it should deserve a state subsidy. But later I learned that the Mickery company was started in 1966 by one man in a barn not far from the city and did not receive support for the 1972 move to its present location until it had demonstrated its continuing appeal to Amsterdammers.

A few days later I went to the little Shaffy Theatre in the Felix Meritis building at 324 Keizersgracht. Felix Meritis—literally "Happy through Merit"—was originally an exclusive society founded in 1777 to promote interest in the Arts and Sciences. In those eager days of the Enlightenment, when new cultural fashions were sweeping through Europe, the society was an immediate success. Its headquarters—a house with slim windows in three tiers and half-pillars supporting a triangular pediment—looked as the Parthenon might have, had it been built on an Amsterdam canal.

Inside there was an observatory, a library, many sculptures and scientific instruments, and a fine concert hall. For a hundred years the citizens of Amsterdam dutifully attended its concerts, admired the statues and dozed through the learned lectures there. Then, as quickly as it had begun, interest in Felix Meritis died; the building was converted into offices and soon nothing was left of its glories.

This state of stupor lasted from the 1880s to the 1960s when, in what must rate as one of the most delayed come-backs in show business, Felix Meritis regained its former vigour. Now those same halls accommodate not only the Shaffy Theatre but everything from movies to children's theatre. Once again the building is packed with people searching for enlightenment, although now they would probably call it Truth or Social Justice. The average age of the audiences is about half that of the original Felix Meritis members, and their belief that the world can and should be made a better place is certainly less smug than once was the case.

Erected by a disgruntled citizen as a memorial to bygone days when Amsterdam was relatively car-free, a flower-bedecked gravestone usurps part of the sidewalk on a bridge across the Singel—an incursion that quickly brought about its removal by the authorities.

There is a very real residue of the Provo and Kabouter period in Amsterdam. Although followers of the counter-culture have widely dispersed, many men and women who came to Amsterdam flying that philosophic banner have chosen to stay. Most days and nights you can find some of these exiles at the Paradiso or the Melkweg (Milky Way), two huge youth centres subsidized by the city and used for films, concerts, dances, plays, meetings and open dealings in soft drugs. The Melkweg, a former dairy plant behind the Municipal Theatre, promotes itself as a centre for the "alternative society". When I paid a visit, I asked a female student how the centre could be "alternative" to the society that was paying for it. She looked at me very sternly and replied: "We are as alternative as you can get in this world. We are true anarchists." It was not the thoughtful answer I hoped for but for me it confirmed once again that these people have indeed convinced themselves that it is possible to accept financial handouts as their due without compromising their ideals.

My visit to the Paradiso was particularly poignant. A former church, it stands only a hundred yards from Leidseplein, directly opposite the Barlaeus, my old high school. We used to hold graduation ceremonies in the assembly hall. I recall sitting there in an almost palpable cloud of pomp and fuss and Latin (and once in anguished embarrassment, when my father made a speech). But now the exterior was painted in psychedelic colours, and purple and orange lights flashed along the walls inside. When I arrived, a young man was lying naked on the floor smoking marijuana.

I lingered in the Paradiso for a while, drinking beer with an artist from England who was neither young, nor naked, nor stoned. He was a serious fellow, in his mid-thirties, I guessed, and he explained that he produced posters and other printed materials in the Paradiso's graphic workshop. He had been in Amsterdam for eight years. Some of the other Englishmen and Americans in the place, he told me, were actors who had worked at the Mickery and decided to stay behind when their tours ended.

My companion certainly did not seem to be prospering, in the tax collector's sense of the word, and he was a bit long in the tooth for his surroundings. As if guessing my thoughts, he smiled and said: "Do you know these kids give pensioners free entry to the Paradiso? Isn't that sweet?"

"Tell me," I asked, "you said you had your own workshop in London. Why did you come to Amsterdam?"

"Because," he answered, "here everyone leaves everyone else in peace."

City on Two Wheels

At the end of the working day, some of Amsterdam's half-million cyclists disembark from a free ferry that carries commuters across the old harbour.

While most cities have become hostages to the internal combustion engine, Amsterdam remains conspicuously devoted to pedal power. Bicycles, equipped with baskets and panniers to carry everything from sandwiches to small children, are the favoured mode of personal transport for two of every three Amsterdammers and account for more than a quarter of all journeys in the crowded city centre. Reasons for the popularity of two-wheeled transport are not hard to find. The bike is ideally suited to Amsterdam's gentle gradients and busy, narrow streets; and in one of the most pollution-conscious cities in the world, its innocuous means of propulsion is considered a particular boon. Loyalty to the lowly cycle extends to rich and poor, young and old alike; even members of the Dutch royal family have taken to two wheels during sojourns in the city.

A child peers from a makeshift rainhood as he and his chauffeur join the two-wheeled traffic along Singel.

In the same impromptu cycle parade, a woman protects a plant under plastic.

Umbrella aloft, a young man pedals by with the poise of a circus performer.

Weighted down by his gear, a workman keeps a careful eye on the road ahead.

Elegant even in rainwear, a young lady goes shopping with perfect aplomb.

Cycling at a sedate pace through Vondel Park, an elderly gentleman and his canine passenger seem the very embodiment of "deftigheid"—a word which Amsterdammers use to sum up the old-fashioned virtues of decorum, propriety, respectability and dignity.

Garlanded with flowers, this bike is a study in two-wheeled eccentricity.

A bicycle that has taken to the trees adds a new dimension to parking.

Ownerless cycles wait to come under the public auctioneer's hammer. City police conduct regular round-ups of two-wheeled strays.

In defiance of an unmistakable sign marking a bicycle lane, parked cars intrude into the cyclist's domain, forcing a rider to take to the open road.

Once someone's trusty steed, a traffic casualty lies discarded and forgotten, its buckled wheels and worn frame collecting rust at a canalside.

An initiate receives a steadying hand from his mother as they ride along a tranquil path where the skills of one generation can safely be passed on to the next.

7

Setting New Courses

In 1975, the city of Amsterdam celebrated its 700th birthday—the natal occurrence having been officially ascribed to a feudal lord's issuance of a deed to local fisherfolk in 1275. The anniversary was exploited with all the relentless ballyhoo that would be mounted by any modern, publicity-conscious city. Streets were decked with bunting and flags, some of which were stolen by souvenir-hunters before the party began. There was a regatta in the harbour and orchestras played in the main squares. A full-scale model of a street scene in old Amsterdam—Mokum, according to the slang name borrowed from the early Jewish community—was installed at an international exhibition hall on Europaplein. Visitors to the exhibition could wander among their counterparts of the 19th Century: street-vendors and barrel-organists; diamond workers, shoe-makers and glassblowers.

In a city steeped in history, it was only natural that the organizers of the anniversary celebrations should lay special emphasis on old traditions. But Amsterdam is a city *with* a past, not *of* the past; modern Amster-dammers are fiercely proud of their heritage, but they are no less attentive to their future. Thus, while the septicentennial offered them an oppor-tunity for a fond look backwards, it also sparked off a debate about the role of the city in the late 20th Century. What new jobs will be created to fill the vacuum left by the decline of old industries and the loss of Holland's trading colonies? What sort of housing will be available in the year 2000? What can be done to combat the worsening problem of air and water pollution? These questions are particularly pressing for a small, crowded city in a small, crowded country; and the debate has only intensified in the years since the septicentennial. Inevitably, I found myself grappling with such concerns during my own investigations of the metropolis.

Any examination of Amsterdam's future must—like any assessment of its past—begin at the sea. When I visited the old harbour shortly after my arrival, a sort of memorial hush had seemed to hover about the docks and quays. My nostalgia in these surroundings was lent a melancholic note by the knowledge that Rotterdam, about 40 miles to the south, had surpassed Amsterdam as the largest port in Holland—and had, in fact, become the busiest shipping centre in the world.

I decided to survey Amsterdam's own modern facilities and, for a guide, I enlisted an official of the Harbour Building—headquarters of Amster-dam's port authorities. He introduced himself as Mr. Pekelharing (this surname, which literally means "pickled herring," is a respected name in

A serried pattern of sunlit shutters relieves the sombre façade of an old brewery warehouse on the Brouwersgracht. Like many former warehouses in Amsterdam, this building has been given new life and purpose after its conversion into an apartment house.

a seafaring community that grew rich on its herring industry). We went by car, because the modern basins, berths and quays are strung out for some four or five miles along the North Sea Canal, which begins at the western end of the old harbour and empties at IJmuiden, 10 miles west of Amsterdam. During the journey, my guide quoted some impressive facts about the waterway. It is almost 300 yards wide, he told me, and about 8,000 tankers and freighters use its facilities. Floodlights are mounted along its entire length so that it can be navigated 24 hours a day; and in winter it is kept open by icebreakers.

The harbour official had supplied me with publicity pamphlets whose gushing prose frequently resorted to the adjective "bustling". But when we reached our destination—a complex of large basins flanked by towering cranes, concrete silos and rows of containers, all set in a desolate area of sandy pastures—I saw that the term was rather misleading. Huge ships were present by the score, but very few people were to be seen. The "bustle" was almost entirely mechanical. We watched a freighter being loaded with soya bean meal through a three-foot-wide pipe connected to a silo. The whole operation was controlled by someone, or something, unseen. A high-pitched whine filled the air, as did the evil-smelling meal, which soon covered our faces with a film of purplish dust.

Mr. Pekelharing led me along a metal catwalk above the quay towards the stern of the freighter. There was nobody on deck. Looking down at the ship's bridge, I was startled by the lack of a helmsman's wheel and of a classic throttle with such notations as "Full Ahead", "Steady" and "Full Astern". Instead, there was a reclining leather seat facing a large console crammed with dials, buttons and gauges. "One captain tried to get his controls changed," Mr. Pekelharing said. "He insisted that any proper bridge should have a helmsman standing behind a wheel. But the ship-owner refused, and who can blame him? To have a wheel custom-built and replace the console would have cost 20,000 guilders ($11,000)."

"Where is that stuff going?" I asked Mr. Pekelharing, pointing to the soya meal that was piling up in the ship's hold. "Probably to Germany," he replied. "Until about 1950 the port served the home trade; now it's principally a transit port, with about three-quarters of the imports destined for other European countries. Most of the freight—mainly metal ores, oil, timber, coal and chemicals—is transported to Germany by barge along the Amsterdam-Rhine Canal."

The latter waterway, opened in 1952, links the port with the German border, about 60 miles away. Mr. Pekelharing's explanation of the connection with Germany ended in a reflective silence. "It's ironic," he said eventually. "Before the Second World War the Germans were our main competitors. We only kept going because they started a war every 20 years and then, after they lost, we had a respite from their competition. Now, they are our biggest trading partners. In fact, half of the yachts that

Lounging on flower carts in Aalsmeer's reception hall, loaders take an early-morning break before the bidding starts in the auction room next door.

A Blooming Business

Ever since the 17th Century, Holland has been a flower growing centre. But the industry's wholesale market-place—the Aalsmeer auction complex just outside Amsterdam—is a model of ultra-modern efficiency. Buyers at Aalsmeer range from local stall-holders to big-time exporters (80 per cent of the cut flowers are air-freighted abroad). Six days a week, they gather in the main hall (overleaf) for a nerve-tingling procedure called a "Dutch auction". Prices, indicated on a computerized device resembling a clock, start high and are progressively lowered by the auctioneer; the first customer to press a button on the desk in front of him stops the price-clock and secures the offered batch of blooms.

In an auction room of the Aalsmeer market, buyers scan the giant price-clocks that register the state of bidding for the flowers displayed below them.

you see on the IJsselmeer belong to industrialists from the Ruhr. They can drive there comfortably in two hours on the motorways."

I drew my guide's attention to an oil tanker that was slowly making its way up the canal. "I never saw a ship of that size in the old harbour," I said. He appraised the vessel with an expert eye. "That's about 50,000 tons; the canal is navigable by ships of up to 90,000 tons. But Rotterdam can handle tankers of 200,000 tons; what's more, it stands at the mouth of the Rhine—a natural barge artery to the heart of Europe. Unquestionably, they have an enormous advantage over us, but I think it's also fair to say that Amsterdam's competitive instincts are second to none."

The rivalry between Amsterdam and other Dutch cities is of long standing. As one of the last great city-states of modern times, Amsterdam was a main protagonist in Holland's 17th-Century struggle for independence from Spain; and its pre-eminence then gave it a sense of importance and independence that has proved amazingly tenacious. Although The Hague is the seat of government and Rotterdam is the greater port, Amsterdam never loses an opportunity to assert its own claims to urban greatness. For example, when Rotterdam decided in 1959 to build an underground railway, Amsterdam immediately began planning its own Metro. When Rotterdam received a grant to expand its port facilities, Amsterdam badgered the national government into giving the city money to modernize its own harbour. Unfortunately, Rotterdam has proved more adroit at getting state support and aid than Amsterdam.

I visited a businessman in his office on the Westermarkt, opposite the Westerkerk. He said, "The reason we don't get more government money is that this city is republican and anarchist."

I looked at him in surprise. He was a thin, middle-aged gentleman conservatively attired in a neat wool suit—a far cry from the wild Provos and their heirs. "Anarchist?" I repeated.

But the businessman wasn't using the word in its political sense. "We're too independent," he explained. "Amsterdam is for ever trying to lay down the law to everyone, including the Prime Minister. You can't do that without causing offence to somebody. I'm not excluding myself," he said. "Our businessmen are republican and anarchist; they may sit in air-conditioned offices these days, but they aren't much different from the gentlemen who ran the East India Company. They're still merchant adventurers at heart, ready to trade with the devil."

The businessman himself dealt in imports and exports, and his firm had once enjoyed a thriving trade in tobacco, sugar, tea and coffee—until the Netherlands lost its overseas colonies after the Second World War. The purpose of my visit was to find out how the man's company had adapted to the collapse of empire. Sitting in his office, it was difficult to believe that anything had changed; the room was furnished in lavish

Crossing the old harbour to North Amsterdam, a ferry boat is dwarfed by the dry-docked tanker behind it. Ship-repairing is one of the city's biggest industries.

art-nouveau style, with Tiffany lamps, walnut and mahogany panelling, and impressively high ceilings and doors—in short, a kind of monument to pre-war prosperity. But my host had the practical outlook of a man whose ideas are tested in the great world outside his windows.

That world, he made clear, has shrunk considerably since the 1930s, when Amsterdam firms monopolized the East Indies trade, controlling the export and sale of 86 per cent of the world's pepper, 37 per cent of its rubber, 19 per cent of its tea, as well as a sizeable proportion of its coffee, tobacco and sugar. "My company is one of the few still involved in tropical plantations," the businessman told me. "We import cocoa, tea, quinine and coffee. A broker in coffee. . . ."

He stopped and we both started to laugh. Every schoolboy who spent his years in Amsterdam before the war knows the sentence: "I am a broker in coffee and I live on Lauriergracht." It is the opening line of a 19th-Century novel—by an Amsterdammer who wrote under the pen name of Multatuli—that won fame as the first articulate broadside levelled at the Dutch colonial system. Unfortunately, the book's message was lost on the home government—at the time of publication and well on into the second quarter of the 20th Century. To maintain its imperial claims in the East Indies after the Second World War, the Dutch mounted two so-called "police actions" against armed independence groups. When the East Indies finally gained independence in 1949, relations between the former colony and the Netherlands were embittered for many years afterwards.

"We should have changed course in 1945," the merchant said. "Because we didn't, the new regime in Indonesia severed most of the old trading links. The plantation owners that supplied my company with tobacco began to export their crop to Hamburg and Bremen. They wanted it to be auctioned in a country with whom they had no previous colonial ties. We tried to recoup by using our tropical experience in other countries. In the 1950s, for example, we set up sugar plantations in Ethiopia." He pointed to a man in an adjacent office. "He has been in Ethiopia. We have hopes for him. But Ethiopia is not Indonesia. Young men like him used to be trained in field work and then posted for years to the same place. They got to know the country, the people, the local traders. Now their work in the tropics is short, uncertain, clouded by political events."

If Amsterdam can no longer rely on overseas lands as an assured and cheap source of trade goods, it has more than made up the loss by manufacturing products at home. On drives around the city I had seen evidence of glowing industrial health everywhere: ultra-modern chemical, electronics and car-assembly plants. The suburbs also offered examples of merchandizing on a truly grand scale. West of the city, near Schiphol Airport, I visited a garment centre, the Confectiecentrum, where more than 200 ready-to-wear clothing manufacturers and agents occupy show-

Presided over by a bronze Mercury, brokers go about their business on the floor of the Amsterdam Stock Exchange. The building, opened in 1913 on Beursstraat, is the fourth securities market-place tne city has had. The earliest, which began quoting share prices in 1611, was the world's first stock exchange.

rooms spread over 15 acres. I also toured the near-by Aalsmeer flower market where, each day, up to 2,000 wholesalers bid for cut blooms and potted plants that are sold all over Europe and North America. Commercial flower growing, of course, has a long history in Amsterdam and its environs. A florists' guild and flower market were established in Amsterdam at the beginning of the 17th Century, and tulips—which grow particularly well in the sandy Dutch soil—were then such a valuable export commodity that the bulbs of some unusual hybrid specimens sold for the equivalent of $10,000 apiece.

Within the city itself, the diamond industry is a model of how a long-established craft can adapt itself to meet the needs of the technological age. Although severely crippled by the forced deportation of some 2,000 Jewish craftsmen during the Second World War, the industry has beaten off competition from the United States, Israel and the Far East to re-establish Amsterdam as the diamond capital of the world. Some of the city's 20 or so workshops still specialize in cutting stones for jewellery. In 1949, 40 years after the Amsterdam firm of Asscher cut the world's largest diamond—the 3,024-carat Cullinan—craftsmen at the Van Moppes factory put on another dazzling gem-cutting display when they shaped 58 facets on the world's smallest gemstone: a jewel weighing only 1/100,000 of an ounce, designed simply as an exercise in craftsmanship. It took three months to cut the stone by hand and polish it with a mixture of diamond dust and olive oil; in the process, the mini-gem was lost eight times and was recovered each time only with the aid of a microscope.

But gemstone production accounts for only a fraction of the diamonds sold by Amsterdam workshops; most of the stones are designed for industrial purposes and are cut by complex machinery, including computer-guided laser beams. (Many gemstones are also shaped by mechanical means, but traditionalists say that stones produced in this way look alike and have no "personality".) The firm of Drukker and Son is typical of the new diamond technology; each year it sells up to five million carats—more than a ton—of diamond dust to industry. The dust is used for polishing articles as diverse as spectacle lenses and the nose cones of supersonic aircraft. The same company also produces stones for cutting edges that chop spaghetti into lengths, hone automobile cylinders, and groove airport runways to prevent aeroplanes from aquaplaning during landings in a rainstorm. Among its most specialized products are gold-plated diamonds weighing about 1/350,000 of an ounce each; incorporated into a telephone circuit for the purpose of conducting heat from transistors, they make it possible to handle up to a quarter of a million conversations simultaneously.

Diamond workshops are a very visible part of the city's economic activities and are visited by thousands of tourists each year. In contrast, Amsterdam's financial services—a major ingredient in its present prosperity—operate behind the closed doors of the Stock Exchange or the anonymous façades of stately canalside houses. The financial community includes no fewer than 400 stockbroking firms and 500 bank outlets— astonishing statistics for a city of fewer than a million people. To find out how modern Amsterdam maintains its centuries-old status as a financial centre, I visited a partner in one of the leading investment and banking conglomerates in the city.

"I think we are more international-minded than other cities," he told me. "Of the stocks and shares quoted on the Exchange, about one-quarter are foreign—including more American shares than on any other European exchange. We attract companies from the Common Market countries because Amsterdam has a good communications network with the rest of northern Europe, and because most Amsterdammers speak at least two European languages besides Dutch. But that is just the beginning. More than 50 Japanese firms have set up business in Amsterdam, and 20 or so are listed on the Exchange."

The banker and I were alone in his office. Every time the doorbell rang, he jumped up and ran down the stairs to answer the door. I don't mean to imply that the banker's behaviour was a sign of a democratic outlook, but it did betoken an absence of pretensions, of *capsones*, which contrasted with the stuffy formality of the financiers I had dealt with during my younger days in Amsterdam.

When I mentioned this, the banker said: "We're less hidebound than we used to be. And we're less stingy, too. Take the Commodities Exchange. Before 1940 there was a rule that from half-past-one to a quarter-to-two, visitors entered free. After quarter-to-two, the doorkeeper rang a bell and everyone who went in, member or not, had to pay an admission fee of 25 Dutch cents (about one U.S. dime). In those days the heads of the various trading firms came to the Exchange themselves. I remember seeing one of them, who was worth millions, gulping down his coffee in a restaurant and running out to beat the bell and save himself 25 cents."

"Yet some Amsterdammers seem to pine for the old days," I commented.

The banker shrugged his shoulders and replied, "I'm all for modernity. Look at this office," he said, gesturing at the elegant, antique furniture. "It's a dinosaur. Canalside houses may be beautiful, but they don't make efficient business premises. Imagine how the staff feel having to climb up and down those narrow, steep staircases all day. If I had my way, we would move to a glass-fronted office with lifts, air-conditioning, and an underground car park and a hotel next door for the customers. In fact, the most efficient premises for an international company would be a soundproof basement under Schiphol Airport."

The banker was voicing one side of a bitter argument that divides Amsterdammers—a struggle, many people feel, for the soul of the city

Schoolchildren enjoy a gardening class in the shadow of the Nieuwendam development in North Amsterdam. Gardening—a part of the child's curriculum from the age of 10—also provides down-to-earth recreation for adult residents of the city's new high-rise buildings.

itself. On one side is the outward-looking, efficiency-minded businessman who sees himself as a member of a world-wide economic skein. On the other side is the person who sees himself first and foremost as an Amsterdammer. He wants to stay within a local community, to deal with people he knows, and to keep free from the hectic pace made possible by modern communications and transport systems, with all their attendant disruptions of the traditional Amsterdam environment.

One of the fiercest battles between these two factions was triggered in 1970 by the city's decision to construct the underground railway system —the Metro. Because the soil beneath the city is waterlogged, the Metro could not be built by conventional tunnelling. Sections of concrete tunnel had to be built above ground and then sunk into the soil—a process that necessarily involved the destruction of buildings on the route taken by the railway. The Nieuwmarkt neighbourhood, part of the old Jewish quarter, was one area to be threatened. Local residents, backed by action groups such as the one that aptly called itself *Lastige Amsterdammer* (The Difficult Amsterdammer), took aggressive counter-measures. They organized a protest exhibition of photographs and wall posters on Leidsestraat to publicize what the Metro would cost in terms of houses demolished and the strain on municipal funds. They occupied buildings scheduled for destruction and held their ground there until police—loudly jeered and barracked by onlookers—evicted them.

In spite of the protests, work on the Metro proceeded, but at a slow rate and with no lessening of the critics' outcry. The first line was not opened until seven years after work on the railway began. It linked the suburb of Bijlmermeer, five miles south-east of the city centre, to the Central Station, located beside the harbour, in the heart of the old city.

Although Amsterdammers love to argue about the proper shape for their city's future, there is one issue on which they agree: the need for more dwellings to accommodate the city's constantly expanding population and to rehouse residents of run-down areas. Amsterdam faces a staggering task of renovation—and not just in the oldest portions of the city. Ironically, some of the heaviest rehabilitation work is being done in apartment-block neighbourhoods that date from only the early part of the 20th Century. Even more ironically, these neighbourhoods seemed to be triumphs of enlightened town planning when they made their appearance.

Their story begins during the First World War. With the future uncertain, private residential construction came almost to a standstill. The Municipal Council decided to seize the initiative in fostering the further development of the city. In 1917 it commissioned H. P. Berlage—the architect responsible for the design of the Commodities Exchange—to devise a layout and set a building style for the extension of Amsterdam Old South, the district south of the Rijksmuseum. The council approved Berlage's plans and, using some of the revenue from income tax, embarked on a massive construction programme. Over the next few years, Amsterdam South put out miles of new streets lined with dwellings built in a style that came to be known as the Amsterdam School.

The architecture of the Amsterdam School is as difficult to describe as it is easy to recognize. Visualize wide streets divided by grassy strips and with four- and five-storey buildings on both sides. They are apartment houses, but a determined—almost fanatical—effort has been made to avoid a square, barrack-like effect. The corners of the houses are rounded and façades are decorated with elliptical shapes. There is a curvy, art-nouveau, small-scale monumentality about the buildings that is often enhanced by stone sculptures decorating the environs.

Berlage's blueprint for Amsterdam South was copied in other parts of the city. During the 1920s, Amsterdam School architecture made its appearance in places as far apart as Hembrugstraat, near the western harbour basin; in North Amsterdam, opposite the Central Station; and in Therese Schwartzeplein, half-a-dozen blocks south of Sarphati Park. Therese Schwartze Square, named for a woman painter who died in 1918, affords particularly splendid examples of the style: each of the houses that surround it is built in a trapezoidal shape, with the top floor narrower than the ground floor. Behind each façade, laid out in an eccentric internal pattern, there are six flats.

At an international congress on city planning held in Athens in 1935, the Amsterdam School was the star performer—although I have a suspicion that part of the fanfare was due to surprise; architects of other

A boat-borne refuse collector skims rubbish from the surface of the Reguliersgracht. Frequent clean-ups are necessary since Amsterdammers tend to use canals for casual rubbish disposal. Even more serious is the pollution resulting from primitive sanitation on many of the city's 2,500 houseboats.

countries had never credited their Dutch colleagues with much imagination. In Amsterdam, however, the style came in for ever-increasing criticism. Detractors called the apartment blocks superficial; and some Dutch architects came to refer disparagingly to the Amsterdam School as "apron architecture" because many of the fancy façades concealed interior designs that were inconvenient for living. I myself am a little biased against the buildings, having lived in one of the less comfortable examples from the age of six to 16.

But whether or not one approves of the Amsterdam School, there is no denying that many of the buildings have not stood up physically to the test of time; the original timber piles that support their foundations are frighteningly shaky. Paradoxically, most of the piles beneath the 17th- and 18th-Century canalside houses are still solid. When I asked city officials why the more recent foundations were deteriorating, I was given a variety of explanations: it could be due to a sinking level of groundwater beneath the newer buildings, which allows air to circulate around the piles and thus accelerates rot; alternatively, the cause could be complex processes of underground suction, unique to these areas, that pull the timbers out of true; or the fault might simply be one of poor workmanship. The later diagnosis would appear best to explain why older buildings are relatively free of the malady.

One spokesman, pursuing the point, blamed the trouble on the French Revolution. He told me that, ever since the craft and building guilds were abolished in Holland during the early 19th-Century French occupation, no decent pile-driving had been done in Amsterdam. (This speaker may have been a member of Holland's Anti-Revolutionary Party: it was established in the 19th Century to combat the ideals of the French Revolution and it is still in existence!)

Whatever the reason for the deterioration of the buildings, Amsterdam is confronted with the problem of placing new foundations under many acres of housing. There is a doomsday schedule: some city blocks are in imminent danger of collapse and need to be restored immediately, while others can hold out for perhaps 20 or 30 years more.

When I drove through some of the threatened areas with an official from the *Grondbedrijf* (Soil Enterprise Board), I felt that I was visiting a city afflicted by a giant, but infinitely slow, earthquake. "Look at that wall," my guide said, pointing at a 1920s apartment block. Squinting at the horizontal stone slabs trimming the facade, I saw that some of them were slightly askew. "Twenty years to go," the official intoned.

When I enquired why the restoration had to be paid for out of public funds, he said, "Most of these apartments are owned by building co-operatives financed by the weekly savings of tenants. They can only pay so much, sometimes no more than a few guilders a week, so we foot the bill for the rest. We also pay to rehouse the residents while their homes are being renovated." I went to see some apartment houses that were being restored. It was a drastic process. One entire block had been gutted and looked like a honeycomb. It was propped up by emergency steel frames while workers drove new concrete piles into the subsoil. Building authorities fell that this new type of foundation will have a lifespan of at least 50 years—but that, of course, remains to be seen.

The Amsterdam School of architecture ended with the Second World War: Erasmusgracht was the last thoroughfare with structures built in this style—and it shows clear signs of further stylistic evolution. There are reminders of earlier trends in the rounded corners topped by towers; but the flat roofs and clean, geometrical lines of the façades anticipate a sort of architecture whose most notable expression can be found in Bijlmermeer—the satellite town served by the controversial Metro.

Ultimately, 100,000 Amsterdammers will live in the Bijlmermeer development. Those already there are housed in 11-storey building strips that, seen from the air, resemble angular "Cs" laid out in an irregular pattern. Each strip contains 2,000 flats on average, and each is separated from its neighbours by wide, grassy spaces. The official brochure is not unjustified in claiming that "a park-like atmosphere surrounds the buildings".

The most striking thing about Bijlmermeer is the seeming absence of parking facilities for the tens of thousands of cars belonging to the residents. There are motor roads, but all are built 10 feet above ground, and they end at large central garages, where tenants pay to park their vehicles. Car owners are not allowed to drive to their front doors; but the farthest apartments are only 450 yards from a garage, and the tenants reach them by walking along enclosed passageways. To travel about the development, the residents of Bijlmermeer can either use the wide bicycle paths, which also provide emergency access for fire engines and ambulances, or they can walk along covered causeways, wide enough for electric delivery vans, that not only join the buildings but tunnel right through them.

Many tenants are less than happy with the curbs that Bijlmermeer's planners have placed on automotive convenience. These discontented occupants have often cited excuses—an elderly or infirm relative, perhaps—which, they claim, make it necessary for them to drive their vehicles along the bicycle paths to their front doors. As far as the visitor can tell, however, few such attempts to gain special privileges have met with success; when I visited the suburb, there was not a car to be seen. More disconcerting, the parkland between the buildings was peopleless, too. Clearly, the "park-like atmosphere" publicized in the handouts did not compensate for the lack of the traditional private garden, with its gardening shed and children's sandbox. But the parkland was undeniably peaceful—a place where mothers, if they so desired, could put their children out to play without worrying about their safety.

At a suburban primary school that specializes in giving individual attention to pupils, a class assembles in front of a colourful version of the tree of knowledge.

To their credit, the planners of Bijlmermeer tried hard to make the high-rise suburb pleasant inside as well as out. The centrally heated, airy, well-designed flats may be unremarkable in other cities, but they are something new in Amsterdam. The designers also made provisions for hobby rooms, nurseries, shops and even guest rooms—all the amenities necessary to achieve their vision of a self-contained community. Yet their efforts have been highly controversial. While Bijlmermeer has been acclaimed by some enthusiasts as a monument to better living, it has also been derided as a ghetto for commuters, as a soulless city that makes no allowances for individuality, and as an arrogant imposition by Big Brother. There is no arguing with one fact on the debit side: while the flats were intended for the medium-to-high-price rental market, a lack of demand forced the authorities to use some units for subsidized housing instead.

Among the tenants who moved into the subsidized accommodations were Surinamers who had been granted Dutch citizenship shortly before their motherland became independent in November, 1975. The first arrivals illegally occupied empty flats at Bijlmermeer; and when later Surinamers flooded in, an entire housing strip was made available to them. Soon this strip became a racial ghetto, with all the familiar by-products of segregated living: vandalism, broken windows and plumbing, and taxi-drivers refusing to take passengers there.

Both the Amsterdam authorities and the tenants made a determined effort to halt and even reverse the decline. The squatters were officially made tenants and given rent subsidies. The entire plumbing and sewage systems were ripped out and replaced by new systems because many more tenants than had been allowed for were living in the buildings. A supervisor and a security staff (all of them Surinamers) were hired. These steps more or less put a stop to the vandalism.

I had a cup of coffee with the supervisor in his flat, a pleasant apartment on the ground floor for which he paid 400 guilders (about $150) per month. He attempted to put the vandalism into its proper perspective. "Those kids who smashed windows and destroyed the plumbing were flown from a South American semi-wilderness to a modern Amsterdam suburb. They were bound to react against the strangeness of their new surroundings. The other day one of them visited me and, when he had left, I noticed that my radio was gone. I didn't run after him. Two days later I saw him at the bus stop and I said, 'When do I get my radio back?' It was on my doorstep when I arrived home."

I may appear to have strayed from my theme of Amsterdam-to-be, but race confrontations could become a part of the future of this city as they already have in many other Western cities. Racial tensions could lead to alienation and to an atomized city where no one is his brother's keeper, just as new high-rise buildings with their identical apartments could lead to a corrosive sense of anonymity. I think that Amsterdammers are aware of the dangers posed by the modern building developments, forewarned perhaps by the breakdown of community relations in other cities that have rapidly expanded and modernized. As for possible racial trouble, I still trust in the Amsterdammers' traditional tolerance, their capacity to absorb new things and make strangers welcome in the community.

On my last Sunday in Amsterdam I visited Vondel Park, where I saw a crowd of Surinamer children from Bijlmermeer throwing stones and empty bottles across a pond at other Amsterdammers who were lying on the grass. I like to think of all children as nice *per se*; let's just say that in this case circumstances had made these youngsters rather unpleasant. They certainly provided a discordant note in that quiet and contented park, but they provoked no very indignant reaction from the people sunning themselves on the grass. For one thing, the children's aim wasn't good; and when they got bored with their target practice, they simply ran off with much whooping and hollering.

But let me end with other images from that Sunday afternoon. The park. On my left, the Milkhouse where by mother sometimes bought me an ice-cream and where a photographer with a box camera and a black cloth used to do a good trade with nannies and their children. On my right, the old Casino, now an avant-garde film library. And in front of me, lawns as smooth as green silk with ponds and lakes bright and glittering in the sun. Unmistakably not a British park (too pastoral), not a New York park (except for the stone-throwing children); definitely a Dutch, an Amsterdam, park. There was little here that would have appeared strange to my parents. They would have been surprised, and then pleased by the girls sunbathing in topless bikinis. They would have disapproved of the stone-throwing urchins.

But the foreign workers walking through this scene would have been new to my parents. All these men were dressed impeccably in cheap suits and ties, sad in their need to look so utterly respectable as a barrier against hatred or rejection. And yet I felt sure that, if they could accept Amsterdam, Amsterdam could accept them. In due course, if they wished, they would become Amsterdammers, and they would behave as well and as badly as Amsterdammers have always behaved.

The Rich Language of Windows

DALE BROWN

Reflections of trees and housefronts in a window by a canal enhance the gentle irony of a lace curtain embroidered with images of canalside houses.

The widespread Amsterdam custom of leaving windows uncurtained night and day has drawn the glances of strangers so often that they have long celebrated the city as an exemplar of openness. Yet, an observant stroll along the city's canalsides and down its streets offers evidence that the practice yields to many variations, wistful or whimsical, conscious or unconscious —confirming once again that Amsterdammers and their ways are not to be captured by broad generalizations. Some glittering panes reflect rather than reveal; a face at a window turns out to be that of a doll rather than a person; "spy" mirrors let residents scan the street below without themselves being seen. But most of all, like the eyes in a face, the city's windows express an infinitude of moods—from the reticence of a shuttered warehouse to the flamboyance of panes lit by the setting sun.

MICHAEL FREEMAN

A voluptuous mannequin gazes alluringly at passers-by from a sex-shop in the city's red-light district.

Demurely offering Eve's apple to passers-by, a carved temptress shares the window of a city bar with advertisements for beer and billiards.

A cat peers out of a window fitted with a "spy" mirror reflecting street activity.

Gazing across the Brouwersgracht from a lushly foliaged apartment, a bald 19th-Century doll looks uncannily like some cult image from the tropical East.

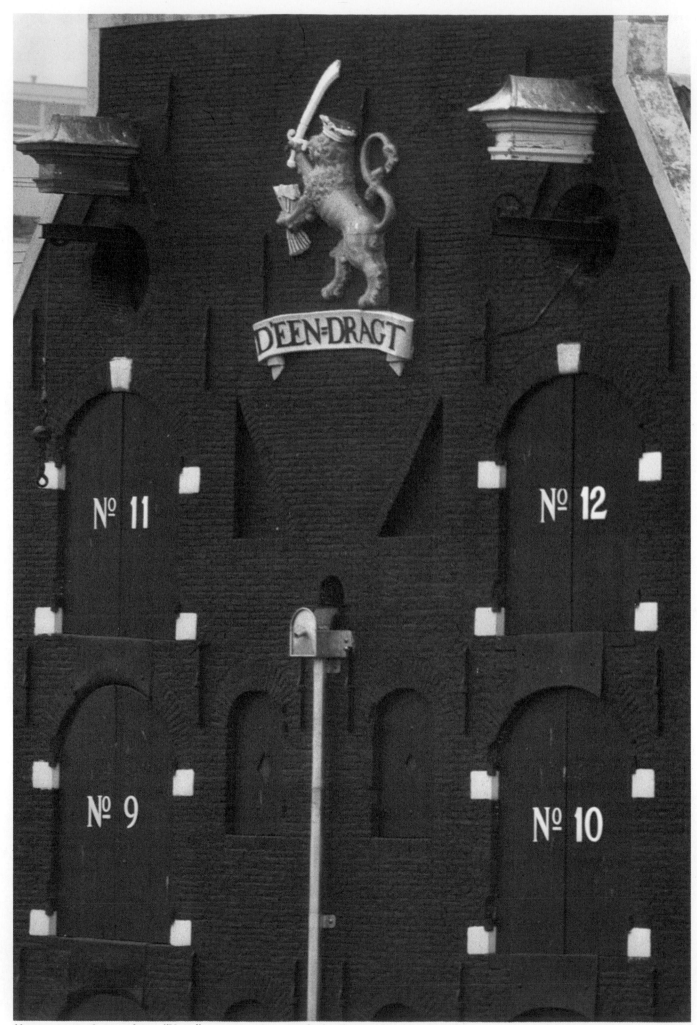

Above a motto that proclaims "Unity", a rampant lion guards the shuttered storerooms of an austerely symmetrical warehouse on Singel.

On a façade near the city centre, an unknown artist has painted windows where none existed, turning a blind wall into a lively peep-show.

As day gives way to night, the moon rises over a row of stately houses before the last reflected rays of the setting sun have drained from the windows.

ADAM WOOLFITT; SUSAN GRIGGS AGENCY, LONDON

Bibliography

Barbour, Violet, *Capitalism in Amsterdam in the Seventeenth Century.* The Johns Hopkins Press, Baltimore, 1950.

Bloom, Herbert I., *The Economic Activities of the Jews of Amsterdam in the Seventeenth and Eighteenth Centuries.* Kennikat Press, New York, 1969.

Boxer, C. R., *The Dutch Seaborne Empire, 1600-1800.* Hutchinson, London, 1965.

Burke, Gerald L., *The Making of Dutch Towns.* Cleaver-Hume Press, London, 1956.

Camus, Albert, *The Fall.* Hamish Hamilton, London, 1959.

Cotterell, Geoffrey, *Amsterdam: The Life of a City.* Saxon House, 1974.

Farber, Jules B., *Amsterdam, City of the Seventies.* De Haan, Bussum, 1975.

Geyl, Pieter, *The Netherlands in the Seventeenth Century.* Benn, London, 1961.

Goudsblom, Johan, *Dutch Society.* Random House, New York, 1967.

Huggett, Frank E., *The Modern Netherlands.* Praeger, New York, 1971.

Huizinga, J. H., *Dutch Civilization in the Seventeenth Century.* Collins, London, 1968.

Kroon, Ben, and van der Heyden, A., *The Glory of Amsterdam.* Elsevier-Phaidon, London, 1975.

Maas, Walter B., *The Netherlands at War: 1940-1945.* Abelard-Schuman, New York, 1970.

Nelson, Nina, *Holland.* B. T. Batsford, London, 1970.

Olie, Jacob, *Amsterdam Gefotografeerd, 1860-1905.* Van Gennep, Amsterdam, 1974.

Rosenberg, Jakob, *Rembrandt: Life and Work.* Phaidon, London, 1964.

Rosenberg, Jakob, Slive, Seymour, and Ter Kuile, E. H., *Dutch Art and Architecture 1600-1800.* Penguin Books, London, 1966.

Shelter, W., *The Pillars of Society: Civilization in the Netherlands.* Martinus Nighoff, The Hague, 1971.

Sitwell, Sacheverell, *The Netherlands.* B. T. Batsford, London, 1947.

Stechow, Wolfgang, *Dutch Landscape Painting of the Seventeenth Century.* Phaidon, London, 1966.

Wallace, Robert, *The World of Van Gogh.* Time-Life International (Nederland) B.V., 1973.

Warmbrunn, Werner, *The Dutch under German Occupation, 1940-45.* Oxford University Press, 1963.

Warners, A., and Wattjes, J. G., *Amsterdam: Four Centuries of Architecture.* Allert de Lange, Amsterdam, 1956.

Weevers, Theodoor, *Poetry of the Netherlands in its European Context 1170-1930.* Athlone Press, London, 1960.

Zumthor, P., *Daily Life in Rembrandt's Holland.* Weidenfeld and Nicolson, London, 1956.

Acknowledgements

The editors wish to thank the following: Tony Allan, London; The Auckland Collection, Hertfordshire; Boudewijn Bakker, Amsterdam; Herman ter Balkt, VVV, Amsterdam; Norman Bancroft-Hunt, Caterham, Surrey; Tricia Chilcot, Netherlands Tourist Authority, London; Charles Dettmer, Thames Ditton, Surrey; Foto Archief, the late Cas Oorthuys, Amsterdam; Sue Goldblatt, London; Daisy Hayes, London; Philip C. Heath, Goodyear Blimp Europa Inc., Rome; F. E. Huggett, London; Hunting Surveys Ltd, London; Jamie Jauncey, London; Dr. Louis de Jong, Rijksinstituut voor Oorlogsdocumentatie, Amsterdam; Michiel Jonker, Historical Museum, Amsterdam; Kodak Ltd, The Hague; Renate Kohler, London; Alan Lothian, London; Russell Miller, London; Monumentenzorg, Amsterdam; Arnoud and Mieke Olgers, Amsterdam; Annelise Smith, Haarlem; Mechie Stormezand, Amsterdam; Dawn Thijm, Amsterdam, Evert Werkman, Amsterdam; Dr. Zwaan, Rijksinstituut voor Oorlogsdocumentatie, Amsterdam.

Engraving on page 52: Frontispiece from Historische Bëschrjvinbe van Amsterdam, Jacob van Meurs, 1663. Courtesy New York Public Library, Astor, Lenox and Tilden Foundations.

Quote on page 46 from a poem by P. C. Hooft in *Poetry of the Netherlands in its European Context,* edited and with translations by Theodoor Weevers, and reproduced by kind permission of the Athlone Press of the University of London.

Index

Numerals in italics indicate a photograph or drawing of the subject mentioned.

Colour reproduction by Irwin Photography Ltd., at their Leeds PDI Scanner Studio.
Filmsetting by C. E. Dawkins (Typesetters) Ltd., London, SE1 1UN.
Printed and bound in Italy by Arnoldo Mondadori, Verona.